Classic Liqueurs

The Fine Art of Creating, Re-creating and
Cooking with Liqueurs

*For Victoria
Enjoy + discover
Cheryl
Long*

Cheryl Long & Heather Kibbey

Panoply Press

New & expanded 5th edition: copyright © 2015 Cheryl Long and Heather Kibbey

Previous editions of this book were published by Culinary Arts Ltd, 1986-1996, and by Sibyl Publications. 2005

ISBN: 978-1-882877-45-4

Printed in USA

Book Design: Northwest Publishers Consortium
Illustrations: istockphoto.com

Cataloging in Publication
    Long, Cheryl,
        Classic liqueurs : the art of creating, re-creating and cooking with liqueurs / Cheryl Long and Heather Kibbey. -- Rev. and expanded [5th ed.].
           p. cm. -- Includes index.
           ISBN 1-889531-06-5

           1. Liqueurs. 2. Cookery (Liquors)   I. Kibbey, H. L., 1944- II. Title.

    TP61 I. L66 2013   641.2'55

Published by:
PANOPLY PRESS
PO Box 1885
Lake Oswego, OR 97035
panoplypress@gmail.com

TABLE OF CONTENTS

TO HOWARD,

who kept us testing
until we achieved perfection!

30TH ANNIVERSARY OF CLASSIC LIQUEURS— CELEBRATING WITH A NEW 5TH EDITION!!

Hard to believe it's been 30 years since we wrote the first edition of **Classic Liqueurs**! Back then, our "Junior Food Testers"—our children— thought there was no higher calling than being required to evaluate dessert recipe after recipe, night after night.

Today they're in their 40s, and that leaves us...well, older. However, don't rush to conclusions that the authors are old fuddy-duddies, with a dusty file of old recipes we haul out every few years. Not at all! Our friendship has endured, as has our love of matters culinary.

This new **5th Edition of Classic Liqueurs** contains all of our well-tested and loved recipes, plus recipes to address new trends in liqueur-making, such as the less-sweet infused brandies.

Cheryl Long & Heather Kibbey
December 2014

THE BASICS OF
LIQUEUR-MAKING

Making and Enjoying Classic Liqueurs

The clear, rich red of Raspberry Liqueur mellowing in its decanter. The luscious fragrances of coffee, vanilla and rum as we stir up a batch of **Old Jamaica Coffee Liqueur,** a taste-alike to **Tia Maria®**. The delight of our friends who receive a gift of **H & C's Irish Cream, Japanese Plum Liqueur, Amaretto-Almond Tea Cake** or elegant **Truffles.** The rustle of paper money in our wallets, saved by doing it ourselves.

All of these are reasons why we make our own liqueurs. And they're also the reasons why the art of liqueur making has been increasing in popularity, year after year.

It's been three decades now since we wrote the books that started it all: *How to Make Danish Fruit Liqueurs* and *How to Make a World of Liqueurs*, published by Culinary Arts Ltd. In those years, we've had the pleasure of meeting and hearing from so many of you who have discovered how much fun it is to create liqueurs of exceptional quality. With the right recipe, it's not at all difficult to duplicate the world's most famous brands or to produce a fruit liqueur of stunning beauty and magnificent flavor.

You'll also find that it's a delicious idea to use liqueurs to flavor beverages and foods, from appetizers to desserts. This book has plenty of recipes to inspire your culinary talents. Don't miss our devastatingly scrumptious **Chocolate Nut Ruffle,** sophisticated **French Country Pâté,** beautiful **Cranberry Jewels in Liqueur,** and many others, all highlighted by the essence of the liqueur. Our recipes allow you to enjoy your favorite liqueurs all through your meals.

This newly revised and expanded 5th edition of **Classic Liqueurs** is the culmination of all our happy years of making and cooking with a delectable handcrafted array of fine liqueurs. So walk with us through the basic steps, then gather the ingredients and begin your course in the creative art of liqueur making.

Cheryl Long & Heather Kibbey

THE BASICS OF LIQUEUR MAKING

Welcome to the wonderful world of liqueur making! It's a pastime that's both easy to learn and produces remarkable results. Discover that there are just a few simple guidelines to make your venture a successful one, so we hope you'll take the time to read this section carefully before you begin.

Unlike the processes of wine and beer making, the creation of a remarkable array of liqueurs requires little or no special equipment. You may have everything you need right in your own kitchen, with the exception, perhaps, of large glass aging containers. (Even then, for many recipes, it's possible to age the liqueur in two smaller 1-quart canning jars or mayonnaise jars.) So you won't need to spend a great deal of money setting yourself up for success.

Unlike beer and wine, liqueurs are very forgiving. If you're ready to go on vacation, for instance, and your liqueur has reached the end of its first aging period, you won't have to cancel your reservations to deal with it. A few extra days or weeks of waiting doesn't harm a liqueur. Isn't it nice to have a hobby that's so undemanding?

That doesn't mean you can throw the rules out the window and expect miracles. But if you start with our easy suggestions and well-tested recipes, you can be assured of good results. In this section of the book, we share with you the guidelines we've discovered after many years of liqueur making. Often, we learned the hard way, through occasionally less-than-perfect batches. We hope that the wisdom we've accumulated through plenty of experience will help you avoid the pitfalls.

Equipment

Making liqueurs at home does not require anything really special in the way of equipment. You will need some, but not all, of the following for each particular recipe:

Aging Containers:

Glass jars with lids (wide-mouth, 1-quart or larger are best)

Ceramic crock with lid

Ceramic bowls, glass bottles and/or decanters with either screw-on lids/caps or cork/glass caps

Strainers:

Metal colander

Fine Wire-mesh strainer

Cloth jelly-bag

White/natural cotton muslin or linen cloth

Cheesecloth

Paper coffee filters

Miscellaneous:

Wooden spoon

Glass or metal measuring cups

Metal measuring spoons

Metal funnel

PREPARATION OF EQUIPMENT

The aging containers of glass or ceramic--never plastic--should be properly cleaned before use. First, wash them thoroughly with baking soda and water (about 4 Tablespoons per dishpan). The containers should be sterilized by either boiling them in water for 15 minutes or putting them through a hot dishwasher cycle without detergent.

TYPES OF EQUIPMENT

Kitchen utensils used for liqueur making, such as measuring cups, funnels, etc. should not be made of plastic. Plastic can impart an "off" flavor to liqueurs. Metal, ceramic or glass are preferred.

Straining is one of the most important steps in obtaining a clear, quality liqueur. A large-holed metal colander will strain large pieces but you will need finer straining material for smaller pieces and for your last fine straining. If cheesecloth is suggested, use several thicknesses and discard after use.

The most efficient fine straining is done with either a cloth jelly-bag or with a clean cotton or linen cloth laid inside a strainer. These cloths may be washed and reused. Some prefer to use disposable paper coffee filters for this step, however they are too dense for some of the thicker liqueurs in this book. We recommend that you test a small amount first if you wish to use this method. Try various strainers to see which you prefer.

BOTTLES AND DECANTERS

You'll need an assortment of clean glass bottles or decanters to hold the finished product. For home storage, wine bottles with metal screw-on tops are frequently the most practical container.

For gift giving, small unusual glass bottles with metal screw-on tops, such as condiment, vinegar and small wine bottles, are excellent. Many interesting bottles can be found in kitchen, glass, gourmet, herb and winemaking shops.

Glass decanters are elegant containers in which to serve or give your special liqueurs.

Good places to find inexpensive decanters are garage or rummage sales and second-hand or thrift shops. Decanters frequently have glass tops with a cork insert. This is fine as long as the cork is clean. Beware of containers that originally contained a non-edible product, such as shampoo or cologne. Even if they are made of glass, they are unsuitable for liqueur making as they can be difficult to clean and may transfer an offensive taste or dangerous residue to your liqueur. Therefore, their use is not recommended.

Plastic containers should not be used when making or storing liqueurs. It is also best to avoid all plastic or plastic-lined caps. The flavor from the plastic can be transferred to the liqueur. An occasional exception is when plastic wrap is laid across a bowl in the early stages or to shield an uncoated metal lid from corroding. For example, canning jar lids are usually coated inside; mayonnaise jar lids are not. If you need to use an uncoated lid, plastic wrap may be used under the lid if it does not touch the liqueur.

Cork stoppers may be used if you wish, but remember that corks allow evaporation and they also retain flavors from previous uses. You may wish to seal the cork with wax, plastic wrap or foil to avoid this.

THE PROOF'S IN THE ALCOHOL

"Proof" is a term used to describe the alcoholic content of distilled liquors, such as those used in liqueur making.

To calculate actual percentage of alcohol by volume in a particular liquor, study the label for the proof, then divide by two.

With this method of calculation, you can see that a 180-proof pure grain alcohol would actually contain 90% alcohol, while a 100-proof vodka contains only 50%.

INGREDIENTS

When making any recipe, remember that the quality of the ingredients used will determine the final result. Surprisingly, the highest-priced ingredients are not always the ones we would recommend, so be sure to read our suggestions before beginning.

There are three main types of ingredients to consider in liqueur making: alcohol, flavorings and water.

Alcohol Bases

Each liqueur recipe includes an alcohol base and there are a number of types to choose from. The two most frequently used are 180- to 190-proof pure grain alcohol and 80-proof vodka. Both are easily obtained at your local liquor store.

Pure Grain Alcohol

Pure grain alcohol is a neutral spirit which will usually be diluted half-and-half with water. It has no taste of its own to interfere with the liqueur flavorings. When purchasing a pure grain alcohol, know that all brands are equal. There is no taste difference between lower- and higher-priced bottles.

Vodka

Vodka, like pure grain alcohol, is a neutral spirit usually made from distilled grains and is an ideal base in liqueur making. However, with vodka, there are definite differences from brand to brand. The purifying and refining processes of the distiller determine the end quality. Good vodka should be colorless and without aroma. It should have no real taste of its own. Take time to find the smoothest vodka in your price range. We prefer 80-proof over 100-proof.

Other Alcohol Bases

The other alcohol bases used in liqueur making are brandy, cognac, American or Irish whiskey, Scotch and rum. These all have pronounced tastes of their own and are frequently used with vodka or pure grain alcohol to add their special flavor. Choose them with care and use them sparingly.

Brandy

Basic brandy is distilled from fermented grape juices. Some brandies are made from other fruits. Avoid "fruit-flavored brandies" if brandy is called for, as they will compete with your flavors. Liqueurs should use a good-tasting brandy, but avoid the rare, aged and costly brandies, which should either be enjoyed on their own or used for making infused brandy liqueurs.

Cognac

Cognac is a very fine French brandy which derives its name from the area where the wine grapes it is made from are grown, Cognac, France. You may, of course, substitute any brandy for cognac, but when we recommend cognac it is for a superior liqueur or infused brandy liqueur.

Whiskey

Whiskey, or "whisky" as the Scotch and Canadian versions are spelled, is almost as varied in taste as rum. American whiskey is generally distilled from rye, wheat or corn. Irish whiskey and Scotch (short for Scottish Whisky) are usually made from malted barley. We have found it best to use Irish whiskey in a traditionally Irish liqueur such as Irish Cream, for more authentic flavor. Wherever this is important, we have indicated it; if not indicated, use a whiskey that is pleasing to your taste.

Rum

Rums are distilled from sugar and molasses. Most are made in tropical countries where sugarcane grows, most notably the Caribbean. The lighter-colored, lighter-bodied Puerto Rican or Barbados rums work well. The Jamaican rums are heavier and sweeter. Take care to match the rum to the type of liqueur. Our best advice is to choose a rum that you find smooth and pleasing.

Other Ingredients

Fruit

Fresh fruits are the most delicate ingredients in liqueur making. It does make a difference when the fruits are picked. If too early, flavors will not be well developed, so choose fruit that is at the peak of its season for best results. Beware of the "stragglers." One piece of fruit past its prime can ruin a whole batch of liqueur. So try to follow the fresh fruit seasons if you can.

Fruit peel, often referred to as zest, should be thinly cut, away from the white portion of the fruit. Citrus fruits should be washed very carefully to remove dust and chemical sprays. Use organic fruit where possible. Liqueurs can be ruined by a mold, spoilage or spray that is present in the fruit.

Dried fruit liqueurs can be made any time of the year. But again, choose fresh quality dried fruits for best taste. Dried fruits can deteriorate with age, but it is a slower process.

Herbs and Spices

Fresh seeds, herbs and spices are frequently called for in our liqueur recipes. Always purchase the freshest and best quality possible. While the more common herbs and spices are available in a supermarket, others such as dried angelica root may not be. Health food stores and herb/spice shops usually carry a wider selection at more economical prices.

In order to release the full flavor of a fruit or seed, recipes will indicate that it be cut open or "bruised." Bruising is a partial crushing of the seed to release the inner flavor to the liquid medium. A mortar and pestle are ideal for bruising, however, a small bowl and the back of a spoon may be substituted.

Glycerin

Pure glycerin is an odorless, colorless, syrupy liquid prepared by the hydrolysis of fats and oils. It is used as a food preservative and is available at drug stores, liqueur and winemaking shops, and some herb stores. We think of it as a smoother. It performs two services: first, it gives additional body to thinner liqueurs that do not have as much natural body as desired.

Secondly, it adds a smoothness or slipperiness in the tasting or sipping of a liqueur that gives it a professional quality. In general, quantities of glycerin will vary, depending upon the need of the individual liqueur. However, we recommend that you do not exceed a few tablespoons per quart of liqueur, except in special recipes as noted.

Sugar & Sweeteners

We recommend the use of cane sugar rather than beet sugar for a number of reasons. The two have slightly different flavors that become pronounced in a liqueur and we've also found that that pure cane sugar produces greater clarity. Then too, the concern that an estimated 90% of sugar beet crops have been genetically modified is also to be considered. You may wish to experiment with other sweeteners, as we do occasionally.

Water

Water quality and taste vary considerably from one area to another. If you have good-tasting drinking water, you may choose to use it in liqueur making. However, for the best quality control in liqueur making, use distilled water. Distilled water will not impart any off flavors and you will receive the fullest taste from your liqueur.

AGING

There is one element in liqueur making that is absolutely essential to good quality and taste: the aging process. We are amazed to find that so many recipes we have seen ignore this step. Aging removes the raw edge of the alcohol, no matter which type of alcohol is used. It lends mellowness and a professional quality to a liqueur that develops only with time. Your homemade liqueur will be quite different from its commercial counterpart if not correctly aged.

We have indicated minimum aging times for each recipe. After this period of time, the liqueur is certainly ready for cooking purposes, but you may choose to age it additionally before drinking. We recommend a taste test at this time.

Except for the refrigerated cream liqueurs, which should be used within 6 months, most of our recipes will be at their peak after one year's aging. Non-cream liqueurs stay at their peak for about 3 years. When you double, triple or halve a liqueur recipe, do not change aging time. An aging time of 2 months, for example, will still be 2 months regardless of the batch size.

SIPHONING

Before the initial straining, most liqueurs have particles of fruit or spices suspended throughout the liquid medium. Careful straining will eliminate these. But some liqueurs, during aging, form a layer of clear, particle-free liquid and a second, cloudy layer. Attempts to strain this merely result in recombining the two layers, producing a cloudy liquid. Siphoning is a much more efficient way to solve this problem.

Use a piece of plastic tubing 20 to 24 inches long. (Beer and winemaking stores carry tubes especially for this purpose.) Place one end of the tube in the bottle of liqueur so that the end is at a level 1/2 inch above the sediment. Bend the tube and suck gently on the other end until the liqueur fills the tube. With your finger over that end, place it in the empty bottle and at the same time, raise the bottle of liqueur so that the layer of sediment is 4 inches or so above the empty bottle. To stop the flow, just lower the full bottle so that the liquid levels in both bottles are the same. When the clear liquid has been siphoned off, discard the sediment.

BRAND NAMES

As you leaf through the recipe section of this book you'll find that some of your favorite liqueurs seem to be missing. For instance, you won't see a recipe labeled "Galliano" because Galliano® is the brand name for that specific commercial product. Legally, we may not use these brand names for our liqueur counterparts, and so we have invented our own names. (Our facsimile of Galliano® is called "Italiano Gold Liqueur," for instance.)

Some names, such as Amaretto and Irish Cream are not brand names, even though we may associate them with one major producer. For these liqueurs, we are legally permitted to use the familiar title.

EQUIVALENT LIQUID MEASURES

3 teaspoons = 1 tablespoon

2 tablespoons = 1 ounce

5⅓ tablespoons = ⅓ cup

8 ounces = 1 cup

16 tablespoons = 1 cup

2 cups = 1 pint

16 ounces = 1 pint

2 pints = 1 quart

32 ounces = 1 quart

4 quarts = 1 gallon

25.6 ounces = ⅕ gallon or ⅘ quart (called a "fifth")

5 fifths = 1 gallon

1 pony = 1 ounce

1 jigger = 1½ ounces

1 dash = 3 drops

METRIC CONVERSION

Liquid Measures:

1 milliliter = .034 fluid ounces

1 liter = 33.8 fluid ounces or 4.2 cups

1 fluid ounce = 29.56 milliliters

1 fluid cup = 236 milliliters

1 fluid quart = 946 milliliters or .946 liters

1 teaspoon = 5 milliliters

1 tablespoon = 15 milliliters

Oven Temperatures:

350° F = 180° C

375° F = 190° C

400° F = 200° C

425° F = 220° C

450° F = 230° C

MAKING
FRUIT LIQUEURS

The art of making cordials, liqueurs or ratafia immigrated to America with its earliest settlers. Secret family recipes were brought to the New World and carefully guarded. Some of these were recipes for fine liqueurs, reserved for formal dining and special occasions. Other recipes were for "medicinal cordials," thought to make anyone feel better.

Fruits, herbs and spices were common ingredients in early liqueur recipes. However, the settlers found that they had to make substitutions for ingredients not found in the New World. But, in substituting, they discovered that many native fruits produced new and tasty liqueurs.

Gracious hospitality in America's early days dictated that guests be greeted with a small glass of sweet liqueur, no matter what time of day they arrived. Liqueurs also provided a relaxing touch when served with tea or coffee after dinner. Often the after-dinner liqueurs were called "digestive cordials."

The custom of using liqueurs in mixed drinks was not popular until the twentieth century. It began in the Prohibition days when smooth, sweet-tasting liqueurs softened rough "bathtub" gin. Later, noted liqueur companies and distillers developed recipes for mixed drinks that became widely popular.

Today, cooks have discovered that fruit liqueurs are a lovely way to capture fresh seasonal flavors. Here in the Pacific Northwest, we never miss a berry season, and we enjoy watching large glass containers of colorful liqueurs age on open shelves in our kitchens. Fall brings apples and pears for other delicious liqueurs, while all year 'round we make batches from non-seasonal or dried fruits, such as lemons, oranges, bananas or dried apricots. So let's get started, exploring the realm of fabulous fruit liqueurs.

APPLE LIQUEUR

Our version of **Applejack**. *Apple liqueur has been made in Germany since the 1700s. Different varieties of apples may be used; each gives its own unique flavor. Apple Liqueur is flavorful and versatile in cooking; add to apple or mince pies for unexpected richness. Ready in 2 months. Makes over 1 quart.*

2½ pounds sweet apples*
2 cups vodka
2 cups brandy
1½ cups granulated cane sugar
¾ cup water

Wash apples and remove stems. Cut into wedges or slices and put into aging container. Pour vodka and brandy over apples, stirring with a wooden spoon. Cap and age in a cool place for 1 month.

Pour liqueur mixture through a fine cloth bag that has been placed into a large bowl. Set bag with apples into another bowl to drain. Clean aging container, removing any sediment. Pour strained liqueur back into clean aging container. Twist top of bag and with the back of a spoon press out any liqueur possible. (Some apples are soft and easy to press, others are hard and don't permit much liquid to be pressed out.) Pour liqueur/juice into aging container.

Combine sugar and water in a small saucepan. Heat, bringing up to a boil, stir constantly. Set aside to cool. Pour strained liqueur and cooled sugar-water into aging container. Cap container and let age at least 1 more month. Liqueur improves with additional aging.

After aging time, check clarity. If any additional straining is needed, do it this time. A fine wire mesh, cloth or coffee filter is best for finer straining. When desired clarity is reached, bottle and store in a cool, dark place.

VARIATIONS:

*TART APPLE LIQUEUR is crisp and refreshing. Increase the sugar to 2 cups and follow recipe and directions. Use tart apples such as Northern Spy, Gravenstein or Granny Smith.

SPICED APPLE LIQUEUR is made by adding two 3-inch cinnamon sticks and 10 whole cloves. Remove spices before pressing liquid from apples. Both sweet and tart apples are good.

QUINCE LIQUEUR can be made quite simply by substituting the apple-like quince fruit for the apples.

APRICOT LIQUEUR

Capture fresh apricots at the peak of the season and make a smooth and fragrant liqueur. Lovely color and taste make it a favorite. Ready in 1 to 2 months. Makes about 1 quart.

> 1½ pounds fresh apricots (about 3 cups), pitted
> 1 fifth vodka
> 2 cups granulated cane sugar
> ½ cup water

Place cut apricots and vodka in aging container; set aside. Place sugar and water in a small saucepan. Heat over medium heat, stirring constantly until sugar is dissolved. Remove from heat and let cool. When cool, pour sugar liquid into aging container. Stir gently to combine. Cap and place in a cool, dark place. Stir weekly with a wooden spoon for 1 month.

Set colander into a large mixing bowl. Pour apricot mixture into colander. Remove fruit; it may be saved and used as liqueured fruit if desired. Pour liqueur through a finer strainer, or unbleached muslin cloth. Discard fine particles. Re-strain until clear. Re-bottle and label as desired. Liqueur is ready but improves with additional months aging.

VARIATION:

ROCK CANDY APRICOT LIQUEUR is made by substituting 1 pound of clear rock candy for the granulated sugar and water in **Apricot Liqueur** recipe. Omit heating. Place candy in aging container with apricots and vodka. Continue as directed. Stir weekly until rock candy has completely dissolved. Proceed as directed.

DRIED APRICOT LIQUEUR

*When fresh apricots aren't available you can still make **Apricot Liqueur**. Dried apricots are excellent as a liqueur base. You get a bonus with the plumped, liqueured apricots after making liqueur. Use them in desserts or compotes, or stuff a pork roast with a mixture of apples, prunes and the liqueured apricots for a special Scandinavian treat. Ready in 1 to 2 months. Makes about 1 quart.*

    1 pound dried apricots
    1 fifth vodka
    2 cups granulated cane sugar
    ½ cup water

Cut apricots in half. Place apricots and vodka into aging container; set aside. Place sugar and water in a small saucepan. Heat over medium heat, stirring constantly until sugar has completely dissolved. Remove from heat and let cool. When cool, pour sugar liquid into aging container. Stir to combine. Seal and place in a cool, dark place. Stir weekly with a wooden spoon for 1 month. Taste and evaluate aging at this time. If more time is needed, allow 2 to 4 more weeks.

Place a colander or large strainer in a large mixing bowl. Pour dried apricot mixture through colander. Remove dried apricots, which are now plumped and liqueured. (These can now be used in a variety of recipes or eaten as is.) Pour liqueur through finer strainer or unbleached muslin cloth. Repeat as needed until clear. Bottle and label as desired. Liqueur is ready but improves with additional aging of 1 to 2 months.

BANANA LIQUEUR

A tropical liqueur that has many uses. Excellent in punches as well as a special ingredient in any banana cake recipe. Substitute rum for the vodka for a more tropical taste. Ready in 2½ months. Makes a little over 1 fifth.

1 large just ripe banana, peeled
1 fifth vodka or light rum
1¼ cups granulated cane sugar
½ cup water
2-inch piece of vanilla bean

Mash banana. Place in a large jar, bowl or crock. Pour vodka over mashed banana. With a wooden spoon push banana below the surface of vodka. (The banana will turn dark brown quickly if exposed to the air.) Cover well to prevent evaporation. Let stand for 2 weeks. Pour through a wire strainer to remove larger pieces of banana. Discard banana.

Combine sugar and water and heat in a saucepan* to dissolve sugar, stir constantly. When dissolved, set aside to cool. Re-strain liqueur through fine cloth (linen, muslin or triple cheesecloth). Strain again as necessary until liqueur is clear.

Add cooled sugar water to strained liqueur. Add a 2-inch piece of vanilla bean that has been slit open. Stir with wooden spoon. Put into jar, bottle or crock and cover well. Let age 1 month, then remove vanilla bean. Do final straining as before, if necessary, for clarity. Pour liqueur into bottle(s) and cap. Let age 1 more month before serving. Can be used without the last month's aging in cooking or punches.

*MICROWAVE DIRECTIONS: Combine sugar and water in a medium microwave-safe bowl or 4-cup glass measure. Stir to combine. Microwave on HIGH (100%) power for 45 seconds; stir and microwave for 30 seconds more; stir again. Set aside to cool and continue as directed.

BLACK CURRANT LIQUEUR

*This spiced dried fruit liqueur is similar to **Creme de Cassis,** a classic ingredient in many gourmet recipes. Keep an extra bottle on hand for cooking. Ready in 4 months. Makes about 1½ pints.*

 1½ cups dried black currants
 2 cups brandy
 1 cinnamon stick
 3 whole allspice
 6 whole cloves
 1 cup granulated cane sugar

Combine all ingredients, except sugar, in aging container. Stir with wooden spoon to combine. Cover or cap tightly and let age for 2 months in a cool, dark place. After initial aging, strain off fruit and spices using a colander or wire-mesh strainer. Set drained fruit aside for another use.*

Pour liqueur back into cleaned aging container, add sugar. Stir well with wooden spoon to dissolve sugar. Re-cap and age at least 2 more months. Shake or stir once in awhile to assist sugar in dissolving. Re-strain through fine strainer or cloth jelly bag to remove any small particles of fruit or spices. When clear, re-bottle and seal. Ready in 2½ months.

* To save the drained fruit for another use, remove spices and refrigerate fruit. The drained fruit may be used in cooking. It's excellent in mince pies.

BLUEBERRY LIQUEUR

A wonderful liqueur that can be made with either fresh or frozen blueberries. This becomes a rich deep-blue colored liqueur. Ready in 3 months. Makes over 1 quart.

> 4 cups blueberries, rinsed and drained
> 1½ cups pure grain alcohol* and 1½ cups water*
> 1 cup water
> 1½ cups granulated cane sugar
> 2 thin strips lemon peel

Place berries in aging container and mash with the back of a wooden spoon (or an old-fashioned potato masher works very well). Add alcohol and then 1½ cups of water to the berries, stirring to combine. Cover container with lid or plastic wrap and let stand at room temperature or cooler for 2 weeks. Stir every few days. If weather is very warm, berry mixture may be put in the refrigerator to avoid mold.

After initial aging, strain mixture over a large bowl through a colander or coarse wire-mesh strainer. Discard fruit residue. Clean out aging container to remove all sediment.

Bring 1 cup water to a boil and pour over sugar and lemon peel. Stir well to completely dissolve sugar. Let cool to room temperature. Remove lemon peel and discard. Pour cooled sugar-water mixture into aging container, add strained blueberry liquid. Stir to combine. Cap and let age 1½ months more.

After second aging, strain mixture through fine strainer, wire or cloth, to remove all sediment. Re-strain as needed until clarity is reached. Bottle and cap as desired. May be used now for cooking, but for serving as a liqueur age at least 1 more month, as it improves with additional time.

*3 cups 80-proof vodka may be substituted for the pure grain alcohol and the water if desired.

VARIATIONS:

SPICED BLUEBERRY LIQUEUR is easily made by adding ½ teaspoon whole cloves and ½ teaspoon whole coriander to the Blueberry Liqueur recipe.

HUCKLEBERRY LIQUEUR is easy, too! Substitute huckleberries for the blueberries in the Blueberry Liqueur recipe. Pick enough on a summer outing to make a batch! They make a wonderful, slightly tart liqueur.

CREATIVE USE OF FRUIT AFTER AGING

When you make a fruit liqueur, the leftovers can be so delicious! This is not equally true of all fruits—bananas, for example, are very unattractive at the end of the aging process.

But many fruits, such as Japanese plums or cherries, retain shape and color, and can be used in a fruit salad or over ice cream, or incorporated in a muffin batter. Just be careful to remove pits or seeds.

CHERRY LIQUEUR

This recipe is exceptionally close to the classic ruby-red **Cherry Heering**® *liqueur from Denmark. Use dark Bing, or other sweet red cherries for the best flavor and color. Traditional Cherry Liqueur uses the cherry pits. We suggest that you do not crack them as some old-fashioned recipes called for, as the cracked pits contain some cyanide. They were used to obtain a hint of an almond taste, however the liqueur is excellent without cracking the pits. Easy to make. Ready in 3 months. Makes about 1 quart.*

  2½ cups vodka
  1 cup brandy
  1½ to 2 cups granulated cane sugar (sweetness to taste)
  1½ pounds red cherries, with pits, washed, no stems

Mix vodka, brandy and sugar in a large glass measure or medium mixing bowl. Stir well to dissolve. Cut each washed cherry slightly to open, leave in pits. Place cherries in 2 sterile, quart wide-mouth jars or 1 larger aging container. Pour liquid mixture over cherries, stir and cap with tight lids. For the first two weeks shake jars several times. Let age in a cool, dark place. Age 3 months, minimum, for best flavor. Strain off liqueur through wire-mesh strainer, discard cherries. Re-bottle as desired.

VARIATIONS:

ALMOND CHERRY LIQUEUR - For a more prominent almond flavor, add 1 teaspoon almond extract to aging container to safely simulate the cracked pits of old traditional recipes. Continue as directed.

NO-ADDED-SUGAR CHERRY LIQUEUR- Substitute 1 cup (8 ounces) apple juice concentrate, undiluted, for the 1½ to 2 cups of sugar in this recipe. Proceed as directed. The "sugars" present will be natural fruit sugars rather than the granulated processed sugars. Taste is excellent; aging is the same.

ROYAL ANNE CHERRY LIQUEUR

While all varieties of cherries can be made into a liqueur, there are differences in flavor, color and sweetness which require recipe adjustments for best results. This recipe is one of the most outstanding variations developed. It has a fresh natural flavor and the exquisite color can best be compared to a golden sunset. Ready in 3 months. Makes about 1 quart.

> 1½ pounds fresh Royal Anne cherries, with pits, no stems
> 1½ cups granulated cane sugar
> 2½ cups vodka
> 1 cup brandy

Wash cherries. Cut each cherry with a knife to open up. Place cherries in aging container. Pour sugar over cherries, stir with wooden spoon to mix well. Pour vodka and brandy over cherry mixture. Stir well to combine and partly dissolve sugar. Cover container and place in a cool place. Stir regularly in the first month to assist sugar in dissolving. Cap and place in a cool, dark place for 2 more months.

After aging, pour liqueur through colander which has been placed in a large mixing bowl. Discard cherries. Strain again through fine wire mesh or cloth until desired clarity is reached. Bottle as desired. May be served immediately but improves with additional aging.

CRANBERRY LIQUEUR

Our version of **Cranberria®** *and* **Finnish Karp***. A liqueur of magnificent color and taste. It will become a holiday tradition for serving and gift giving. Excellent in punches and cooking. Fresh or whole frozen cranberries may be used in this recipe. Ready in 5½ months. Makes about 1 fifth.*

> 4 cups (one 12-ounce bag) cranberries
> 2 to 2½ cups granulated cane sugar
> 1 cup pure grain alcohol* and 1 cup water*
> ½ cup water

Rinse and check cranberries, discarding soft or spoiled berries. Remove any stems. Chop very coarsely. (A food processor does this quickly and easily.) Place chopped cranberries in aging container(s). Pour sugar over cranberries; pour liquids in next. Stir well with a wooden spoon. Cap and store in a cool, dark place. Stir once a week for 2 weeks. Age 8 weeks longer.

After initial aging, strain through metal colander. Discard cranberries. Return liqueur to aging container. Let age 3 months longer. Re-strain through fine strainer or cloth to remove any particles or seeds from cranberries. Bottle as desired.

* 80-proof vodka may be substituted for the pure grain alcohol and the 1 cup water in this recipe.

VARIATIONS:

CRANBERRY RUM LIQUEUR - Substitute 2 cups rum for the grain alcohol and water in this recipe for a liqueur with rich rum undertones.

NO-SUGAR ADDED CRANBERRY LIQUEUR - Substitute 1 cup (8 ounces) apple juice concentrate, undiluted, for the 2 to 2½ cups granulated sugar in this recipe. Proceed as directed, but final aging can be decreased by 1 month. The "sugars" present will be natural fruit sugars rather than the processed granulated sugars. Taste will be slightly more tart but delicious.

CRÈME DE PRUNELLE

This liqueur is our reproduction of a French liqueur that is made from a variety of a wild purple plum known as prunelle. While we thought that it would be a good liqueur, we were surprised it turned out to be a great liqueur! Any variety of dried prunes may be used in this recipe. We have noted subtle differences in the liqueur depending upon the flavor, sweetness and quality of the prunes used. Excellent in meat recipes, especially pork, as well as for sipping. May be made at any time of year. Ready in 3 months. Makes about 1 quart.

> 1½ pounds dried pitted prunes, cut into halves
> 1½ cups granulated cane sugar
> 2¼ cups vodka
> 1½ cups brandy

Place cut prunes in aging container. Add sugar, vodka and brandy, stirring well to combine. Cap and place in a cool place for one month. Stir weekly to dissolve sugar.

After initial aging, pour liquid through a wire strainer placed over a large mixing bowl. Press liqueur juices from prunes with the back of a wooden spoon. Remove prunes from liqueur. Prunes may be saved for cooking. Re-strain liqueur using finer straining material until desired clarity is reached. Bottle as desired. Age 2 more months for best flavor before serving.

VARIATION:

SPICED CRÈME DE PRUNELLE is an easy variation of this French favorite. Just add a 3-inch cinnamon stick and 8 whole allspice to the initial ingredients. Let age as directed and remove spices at first straining. Proceed as directed.

ELDERBERRY LIQUEUR

Wild or cultivated elderberries may be gathered for this delicate liqueur. When picking the berries, use the blue-berried variety. It's important to choose completely ripe berries and to avoid including leaves, stems, flowers or unripe berries, as these can be toxic. Makes about 1 quart.

    8 cups ripe elderberries
    1 cup pure grain alcohol and 1 cup water
    1 cup water
    1½ cups granulated cane sugar
    3 strips lemon peel, each 1-inch long
    3 tablespoons glycerin

Remove all elderberry leaves, stems and debris, wash carefully. Drain off any excess water from berries then pat with dry towel. Add cleaned berries to aging container and mash to open berries. Add pure grain alcohol and 1 cup water, stirring to combine. Cover with lid or plastic wrap and let stand at room temperature for 2 weeks, stirring several times.

After initial aging, strain mixture over a large bowl through a colander or wire-mesh strainer. Discard fruit residue. Clean aging container, removing all sediment. Pour strained elderberry liquid back into aging container through fine strainer to remove all sediment, restrain if necessary, then cover.

Bring 1 cup water to a boil in a saucepan. Add sugar and lemon peel, stirring to combine. Turn heat to low. Continue stirring until sugar is completely dissolved. Remove from heat. Cover and let cool. When completely cooled, remove lemon strips. Pour sugar syrup into aging container, stirring to combine with strained elderberry liquid. Stir in glycerin. Cover and age 1½ months, then re-strain and bottle as desired. Place in a cool dark place for additional aging of at least 1 month.

HAWAIIAN FRUIT LIQUEUR

The tropical islands of Hawaii boast huge pineapple plantations. Sweet, juicy pineapples blended with ripe bananas and laced with Hawaiian rum form the basis for this truly luscious liqueur. You will find it a versatile performer in any mixed drinks, punches and foods. Ready in 2 months. Makes over 1 quart.

> 3 large bananas, peeled
> 2 cups fresh-cooked or canned pineapple chunks in unsweetened
>   juice; drain and reserve juice
> 1 fifth light rum
> 1¼ cups granulated cane sugar
> 1 cup pineapple juice (reserved)
> 3-inch piece vanilla bean
> 6 drops yellow food coloring

Mash banana. Quickly combine banana, pineapple chunks and rum in an aging container.

In small saucepan, combine sugar, reserved juice and vanilla bean. Bring to a boil. Boil for I minute, stirring constantly. Cool to lukewarm. Add the sugar syrup to the fruit and rum mixture; stir to mix well. Cover and let stand in a cool, dark place for 1 month, stirring at least once a week.

After initial aging, strain through colander into a large bowl. Press fruit with potato masher or back of wooden spoon to obtain juice. Discard the fruit and vanilla bean. Re-strain the liqueur several times, using progressively finer filtering material until maximum clarity is achieved. Return to aging container or bottle. Add food coloring; mix well. Age for 1 month, minimum, before serving. If sediments form at bottom of bottle, re-strain and re-bottle.

CALIFORNIA LEMON LIQUEUR

*Our version of **Dopio Cedro**®, reminiscent of the popular Italian lemon liqueur, is one of our personal favorites. Refreshing and excellent to sip, it's a natural in punches and many cocktails, and superb in cooking and baking. Makes about 1 fifth.*

2 large lemons
water as needed
2 cups granulated cane sugar
2 cups vodka

Rinse lemons and pat dry. Thinly peel zest (thin outer layer) strips from lemons. Do not include whiter inner peel. Place zest strips into medium saucepan. Cut lemons in half and squeeze juice into measuring cup. Remove any seeds. Measure juice and add enough water to bring to the 1 cup mark. Pour lemon juice mixture into saucepan with zest, add sugar and stir. Bring mixture to a boil, stirring frequently. When it reaches a boil, reduce heat and simmer for 10 minutes. Remove from heat and cool.

Pour lemon mixture into aging container, add vodka and stir. Cap and age for 4 weeks in a cool, dark place.

After initial aging, pour through metal strainer into bowl to remove zest. Lemon peel may be saved for use in cooking, if desired. Pour liqueur back into cleaned aging container for an additional month of aging.

When aging is completed, strain liqueur through fine cloth (such as muslin) which is placed over a large bowl. Repeat as needed. A cloudy layer may form on top even after several strainings. The cloudy portion may be poured off and reserved for cooking if desired. Bottle and cap as desired.

Liqueur is now ready to be used in cooking but is better for drinking after an additional 3 months' aging.

VARIATION:

LIME LIQUEUR is not only deliciously tart to sip, but is also a versatile ingredient to use in cooking. You'll find that it's excellent with fish and wonderful in salad dressings.

To make Lime Liqueur, substitute the juice from 2 large or 3 medium green limes for the lemons in the recipe above. Since limes can be difficult to zest, use the entire peel (green, white and inner membrane) from ½ lime in place of the lemon zest. Follow remaining directions for California Lemon Liqueur.

TONY'S KEY LIME LIQUEUR

Think of palm trees, sunny beaches and daiquiris! The tiny sweet yellow limes from Florida's Keys are available seasonally coast-to-coast. It's an absolutely marvelous sipping pleasure! Makes about 1 fifth.

> 2 cups granulated cane sugar
> 1½ cups vodka
> ½ cup light rum
> 6 Key limes, thinly sliced

Combine all ingredients in an aging container, stirring well. Cover and age for one month in a cool, dark place. Stir occasionally during the first 2 weeks, until sugar is fully dissolved.

After the initial 1-month aging period, pour liqueur through a colander set in large mixing bowl. Discard fruit. Strain again through a muslin bag or several layers of cheesecloth, until desired clarity is reached. Pour into a bottle or decanter and age in a cool, dark place for an additional 2 months. A slightly cloudy layer may form as the liqueur ages, but this may be gently poured off and used in cooking.

LOVE POTION LIQUEUR

This classic violet-colored French liqueur, known as **Parfait d'Amour** *was once used as a love potion. Ready in just 2 weeks. Makes about 1 quart.*

1 teaspoon lemon extract
¼ teaspoon orange extract
3-inch piece vanilla bean or ¼ teaspoon vanilla extract
4 to 6 flower petals: rose, pansy or violet (optional)
3½ cups vodka
½ cup brandy
1½ cups granulated cane sugar
¾ cup water
1 teaspoon glycerin
3 drops red food coloring (optional)
1 drop blue food coloring (optional)

Combine extracts, vanilla bean, flower petals, vodka and brandy in a 1½-quart or larger aging container. Cap and let age for 2 weeks in a cool, dark place. Strain liqueur through a wire-mesh strainer. Clean out aging container. Return liqueur to container.

In a saucepan combine sugar and water. Bring to a boil, then turn heat down, stirring constantly until sugar is dissolved. Set aside to cool. When cool, add sugar-water to liqueur, stirring to combine. Add glycerin and food coloring if desired. Let stand 24 hours before serving.

TROPICAL MANGO LIQUEUR

The taste of a ripe, fresh mango is exquisite and this lovely liqueur captures it well. The leftover fruit can be saved for use in salads, beverages, chicken or pork dishes, or desserts. Makes about 1 quart.

3 large ripe mangos, peeled and chopped*
juice from 2 lemons (about ⅓ cup)
2 cups granulated cane sugar
1½ cups vodka
½ cup light rum

Combine all ingredients in an aging container, stirring well. If seed is intact and covered in mango flesh, it may also be added to the container.

Cap and age in a cool, dark place for just 2 weeks, stirring occasionally in the first week to help dissolve sugar.

After aging, pour liquid through colander that has been placed in a large mixing bowl. Discard fruit or save, refrigerated, for use in food recipes. Strain liqueur through cloth until desired clarity is reached. Pour into bottle or decanter and age an additional month for best flavor.

OLD-FASHIONED DRIED FRUIT LIQUEUR

"Simple to make and simply delicious" best describes this wonderful liqueur. It offers a bonus of liqueured fruits that are plumped, brandied and ready for topping ice cream, frozen yogurt, pound cake or your favorite dessert creation. Most dried fruits may be used in this recipe; our favorites are apricots, peaches, pears, pineapple, and prunes. Ready in 1 month. Makes about 1 fifth.

> 1 pound dried fruit of choice
> 1 bottle (750 ml) or 3 cups dry white wine
> 1 cup brandy
> 1½ cups granulated cane sugar
> ½ cup water

Place dried fruit, wine and brandy in aging container. Stir gently, Cover and set aside.

Combine sugar and water in small saucepan. Heat gently, stirring constantly. Remove from heat when sugar has dissolved. Let cool. Add cooled sugar mixture to dried fruit mixture, stirring to combine. Re-cover and place in a cool place for 1 month, stirring occasionally.

After aging, strain off fruit by pouring mixture through a metal colander that has been placed over a large bowl. Save fruit for serving. Re-strain liqueur through fine wire strainer or cloth to remove fine particles. Strain until desired clarity is reached. Bottle as desired.

ORANGE CURAÇAO LIQUEUR

This liqueur is named after the Caribbean island of Curaçao where Spanish citrus groves were first planted. Bitter or sweet oranges may be used to make our natural liqueur. Curaçao may also be tinted blue, green or a dark orange with food colors, to resemble commercial brands. Makes 1 fifth.

> 4 large oranges
> 1 teaspoon whole coriander seeds
> 1 cup pure grain alcohol and 1 cup water
> 2 tablespoons orange juice (from oranges above)
> ⅔ cup granulated sugar
> ⅔ cup water

Place cake rack on cookie sheet. Turn oven to warm or lowest temperature. Thinly peel the zest from oranges, using a swivel-bladed peeler or orange zester. Place peel on cake rack. Put in oven and leave until dry, about 1 hour. Let cool before continuing with recipe.

Crush coriander seeds coarsely with a pestle or back of a spoon in a mortar or bowl. Place seeds in aging container. Add dried zest, pure grain alcohol and the 1 cup water to the seeds. Squeeze fresh oranges and measure 2 tablespoons juice. Add to the aging container. Stir to combine. Cap and let age for 1 to 2 weeks, shaking once or twice.

After initial aging, prepare sugar syrup. Combine sugar and ⅔ cup water in small saucepan. Bring to a boil, turn heat down and stir continuously until all sugar is dissolved. Remove from heat and let cool.

Strain orange mixture by pouring through cloth bag placed in a strainer over a large bowl. Rinse out aging container. Pour strained liqueur back into aging container. Add cooled syrup to liqueur. Cap and let age in a cool dark place for 3 to 4 months.

DANISH ORANGE LIQUEUR

A fresh, natural tasting liqueur that is excellent for cooking and baking. Especially good with chocolate. May be used when young for cooking and baking but it is best for sipping with full aging time. Ready in 3 to 6 months. Makes over 1 quart.

> 4 large, sweet oranges
> water as needed*
> 1½ to 2 cups granulated cane sugar
> 1 cup pure grain alcohol** (180 to 190-proof), mixed with 1 cup water*

Rinse oranges and pat dry. Thinly peel zest (thin outer orange skin) from one orange. (Do not peel into the white part of the orange skin, as it is bitter.) Cut up peel into small strips and place in a medium saucepan. Cut all oranges in half (including the one that has been peeled). Squeeze juice into a 2-cup measure, *add water if needed to bring up to that mark. Pour the 2 cups juice (or juice + water) into saucepan with zest; add sugar and stir. Bring up to a boil, stirring frequently. Immediately reduce heat and simmer for 10 to 12 minutes, stirring often. Remove from heat and cool.

Pour cooled orange juice mixture into aging container(s), add alcohol and water, stir to combine. Cap and let age at room temperature or cooler for 3 months.

After initial aging, strain liqueur mixture through a colander to remove the peel. (Discard peel or save for use in a food recipe.) Re-strain through cloth until particles and sediment have been removed. Bottle and cap as desired. Continue aging for 3 more months.

**Substitute 2 cups 80-proof vodka if preferred, in place of the pure grain alcohol and water.

MICROWAVE DIRECTIONS: Substitute a large microwave-safe mixing bowl for the saucepan. Microwave juice mixture on HIGH (100%) power for 4 to 5 minutes or until mixture comes to a boil; stir occasionally. After boil has been reached, reset to MEDIUM (50%) power and microwave for 8 to 10 minutes longer; stir every 2 minutes. Cool and continue as directed.

VARIATION:

ISLAND-HOPPING ORANGE LIQUEUR - Substitute 2 cups of rum for the pure grain alcohol and water in the **Danish Orange Liqueur** recipe.

FRESH PEACH LIQUEUR

Like summer in a peach orchard! A natural, fruity liqueur that can be made any time of year, but fresh local peaches of any variety give the finest flavor. After the liqueur is strained, save the peaches for use in a delicious ice cream parfait or sundae! It's ready in just over 1 month. Makes about 1 fifth.

> 1½ pounds peaches
> 1 cup granulated cane sugar
> 4 strips lemon peel
> 2 cups vodka

Peel, pit, and slice peaches. Place in saucepan.** Sprinkle sugar over the fruit, stirring to combine. Over low heat, warm the mixture until the sugar is thoroughly dissolved and peaches are juicy.

Cool to room temperature. Place peach mixture into aging container. Add lemon peel and vodka, stirring to combine. Cover container and let stand in a cool, dark place (refrigerate if necessary) for 1 week, stirring occasionally.

Strain liqueur mixture through medium wire strainer placed over a large mixing bowl. Press the fruit with the back of a wooden spoon to release the liqueur liquid. Discard peach pulp. Re-strain through finer wire-mesh or cloth until desired clarity is reached. Bottle as desired. Liqueur is fine for cooking at this point and is drinkable, but will improve with further aging.

MICROWAVE DIRECTIONS: Place peaches and sugar into large microwave-safe mixing bowl. Stir to combine. Microwave on HIGH (100%) power for 6 to 7 minutes, stirring every 2 minutes. Proceed as directed.

VARIATION:

SPICED PEACH LIQUEUR, our version of Southern Comfort®, is made by substituting a good quality bourbon for the vodka and adding 2 cinnamon sticks and 4 whole cloves to this recipe. Remove spices on first straining.

GOLDEN PEAR LIQUEUR

Delicate pears of any variety produce this golden liqueur. Use ripe but not over-ripe pears for best flavor. Makes a generous quart.

2½ pounds fresh ripe pears (about 5 to 6 pears)
2½ cups granulated cane sugar
3 cups vodka
1 cup brandy
2 tablespoons glycerin

Trim stem tops and bottoms from washed pears. Stand pear on bottom and cut into eights lengthwise. Remove seeds. Place pears into large aging jar. Add sugar, vodka and brandy. Stir to combine. Cover and place in a cool, dark place for 1 month. Stir weekly.

After initial aging, stir to make sure all sugar is dissolved and strain through colander into large bowl. Discard pears. Clean aging container and strain liquid through fine wire strainer or cloth back into aging container. Age an additional month.

Re-strain after second aging through cloth to remove all particles. Add glycerin and pour into bottles as desired, cap and label. The liqueur is quite drinkable at this point, but improves with another month of aging.

PINEAPPLE PLANTATION LIQUEUR

Fresh ripe pineapples flown in from pineapple plantations make this liqueur available no matter where you live. The pineapple needs to be cooked as directed for a superior liqueur—a real tropical delight! Makes about 1 quart.

  1 fresh ripe pineapple
  ½ cup water
  1½ cups rum, light or dark
  1 cup vodka
  1 tablespoon lemon juice
  1- to 2-inch piece vanilla bean, cut in half lengthwise
  1 cup granulated cane sugar
  ½ cup water
  2 tablespoons glycerin

Cut top and bottom off pineapple. Prepare for eating, removing outer skin. Cut in quarters length-wise. Slice away tough inner core and discard. Lay quarters down and cut about ½-inch or less thick slices. Place pineapple slices and ½ cup water into saucepan. Cook over medium heat for 10 minutes, stirring occasionally. Remove from heat and let cool.

When cool, place pineapple and liquid into large aging container, then add rum, vodka, lemon juice and vanilla bean. Stir.

Pour sugar and ½ cup water into saucepan and heat over medium heat stirring constantly until sugar begins to dissolve. Reduce heat to low and stir until sugar is dissolved. Remove from heat and let cool. When sugar water has cooled, add to pineapple mixture, stirring to combine. Cover aging container and place in a cool dark place for 1 month.

After initial aging, strain liqueur mixture through colander into a large bowl. Save pineapple,* remove vanilla bean. Clean aging container and pour liquid through a fine wire strainer or cloth back into aging container. Place in a cool, dark place for 1 month.

After the second aging re-strain through fine screen or cloth to remove particles. Add glycerin and pour strained liqueur into bottles, cap and label. Quite drinkable at this point but improves with another month of aging.

*The pineapple slices from the rum mixture are delicious in tropical drinks, punches, fruit salads, upside-down cakes, or on ice creams or sorbets.

PIÑA COLADA LIQUEUR

*The Piña Colada cocktail has made this liqueur famous. Made with white Caribbean rum aged in oak casks, **Piña Colada Liqueur** will bring back memories of white beaches, crystal waters and tropical sea breezes at a moment's notice. Ready in 2 to 3 months. Makes approximately 1 quart.*

1½ cups water
1½ cups granulated cane sugar
2 cups packaged flaked coconut
1 vanilla bean, split lengthwise
24 chunks (approximately 1¼ cups) fresh-cooked or canned unsweetened pineapple, drained
3 cups light rum

Bring water and sugar to a boil. Reduce heat to low; add coconut and vanilla bean. Simmer 5 minutes, uncovered, stirring frequently. Remove from heat; add pineapple. Cool to lukewarm. Add rum. Place in aging container and let stand for 1 month, shaking or stirring once a week.

Pour through a fine wire-mesh strainer into a large bowl. Press coconut and pineapple with potato masher or the back of a wooden spoon to obtain all the juice. Remove fruit. Strain liqueur through fine cloth or paper coffee filters several times until desired clarity is reached. Bottle and age an additional 1 to 2 months. If there is sediment at the bottom of the bottle, a final straining or siphoning may be needed at this time. If you prefer, the bottom cloudy layer may be saved for cooking.

PLUM LIQUEUR

Delicious with any type of fresh plums! Each variety gives its own distinctive flavor. Ready in 2 months. Makes about 1 quart.

    2 pounds plums
    2 cups granulated cane sugar
    2 cups vodka
    ½ cup brandy

Wash plums and pat dry. Cut plums in halves or smaller; pit. Place plums in aging Container. Pour sugar over plums; stir. Add vodka and brandy, stirring to partly dissolve sugar. Cap container and place in a cool, dark place for 2 months; stir occasionally.

Place strainer over large bowl and strain liqueur. Press liquid from plums with the back of a wooden spoon. Discard plum pulp. Re-strain liqueur through cloth until clear. Bottle as desired. Ready for cooking or drinking but best if aged another month.

JAPANESE PLUM LIQUEUR

So outstanding in aroma, taste and color, this liqueur is a favorite in our liqueur classes. Japanese Plums are tiny tart fruits on the distinctive purple-leaf landscape trees. Its pits are large, so the plums are often left for birds to enjoy. This recipe, however, requires no pitting and is very easy to make! Ready in 3 months. Makes over 1 quart.

    2 pounds Japanese plums
    2¼ cups granulated cane sugar
    2¾ cups vodka
    1 cup brandy

Wash plums and pat dry. Cut each plum with knife to open, but do not pit. Place in a large aging container. Add sugar, vodka and brandy to plums.

Stir to combine. Cover, let age 3 months in a cool, dark place; stir monthly.

After initial aging, strain mixture through wire-mesh strainer over large mixing bowl. Press out liqueur in plums with back of a wooden spoon. Discard plums. Re-strain through cloth until clear. Bottle as desired. Liqueur is ready to serve but as with most liqueurs, it improves with additional aging.

VARIATION:

GOLDEN PLUM LIQUEUR - This recipe is excellent for small gold plums such as the Mirabelle variety. Liqueur will be golden in color.

ENGLISH DAMSON PLUM LIQUEUR

No English kitchen would be without Damson plums. They are eaten fresh or put into jams, conserves and full-bodied English liqueurs. Agatha Christie's "Miss Marple" serves up this tradition for her favorite guests. We're certain she'd approve of and appreciate this recipe. The liqueur is perfect in Trifle recipes too. Ready in 4 months. Makes about 1 quart.

2½ pounds Damson plums, washed, pitted and halved
1½ cups granulated cane sugar
1 cup pure grain alcohol
1 cup water
⅔ cup brandy

Place prepared plums in a large aging container. Sprinkle sugar over plums and mix gently with a wooden spoon. Pour alcohol, water and brandy over mixture; stir gently. Cap and place in a cool, dark place. Stir regularly for the first month, or until sugar is dissolved.

After sugar is dissolved, strain mixture through a colander placed over a large mixing bowl. With the back of a wooden spoon, press out juice from plums. Plums may be discarded or saved for a cooking use if desired. Re-strain liqueur through fine wire mesh or cloth until desired clarity is reached. Rebottle as desired. Best if aged an additional month before serving.

POMEGRANATE LIQUEUR

A delicate liqueur with a jewel-like color and a gourmet taste. Truly outstanding. Ready in 2 months. Makes about 1 fifth.

2 to 3 large ripe pomegranates
¾ cup water
1 to 1½ cups granulated cane sugar, to taste
2 cups vodka or light rum
2 tablespoons glycerin

Cut pomegranates in quarters. Pull back and remove one membrane at a time, exposing clusters of juicy red seeds. Gently pull seeds away from white centers. Place all seeds in aging container. Discard white membranes, centers and peels. Crush seeds slightly with back of a large wooden spoon.

Heat water and sugar together, stirring frequently, until well dissolved. Let cool. Pour vodka and sugar-water over seeds. Stir and let cool. Cap and place in a cool, dark place. Let age 1 month.

After initial aging, strain through a fine wire-mesh strainer. Discard seeds. Clean out aging container. Place strained liqueur into container. Add glycerin. Age at least 1 more month. Re-strain through cloth, until clear. Re-bottle as desired.

RASPBERRY LIQUEUR

Our version of **Liqueur de Framboise** *is adored for its magnificent color and taste! Make it once and you'll make it again. This recipe also works well with most all cane berries, such as Blackberries, Loganberries, Marionberries, etc. Ready in 3 months. Makes over 1 quart.*

   1 pound fresh raspberries*
   2 cups water
   2 cups granulated cane sugar
   2 cups pure grain alcohol **mixed with 2 cups of water

Rinse and check raspberries, discard any over-ripe or moldy berries. Place raspberries into large bowl. Crush berries slightly with back of wooden spoon. Set aside.

Warm 2 cups of water with sugar in medium saucepan over moderate heat. Stir continuously until well dissolved and liquid is warm. Pour sugar-water over raspberries, stir. Cover with plastic wrap and refrigerate for 1 week. Stir occasionally.

After refrigerator aging, strain mixture through fine wire-mesh strainer into a large bowl or aging container. Add alcohol and additional water; stir. Cap and let age 1 month.

Strain through cloth until clear. Re-bottle as desired. Ready for use in cooking at this point but age 2 months or longer before drinking.

**4 cups 80-proof vodka may be substituted for the 2 cups pure grain alcohol and 2 cups water. Proof of liqueur will be slightly less.

VARIATIONS

*BERRY LIQUEUR - Use this same recipe for all types of cane berries such as Blackberry, Boysenberry, Loganberry, Marionberry, etc.

RHUBARB LIQUEUR

Don't pass this one by! It is delicately colored and captures the fresh rhubarb essence. Delightful for sipping and add some of this rosy liqueur to your next rhubarb pie. Delicious! Ready in 2 months. Makes about 1 quart

   4 cups fresh rhubarb
   3 cups granulated cane sugar
   3 cups vodka

Wash and trim rhubarb. Slice rhubarb about ¼-inch thick by hand or in the food processor. Place rhubarb in aging container. Add sugar and stir. Pour vodka over mixture and stir again. Cap or cover and let sit at room temperature for 2 to 4 weeks. The color will change to a rosy glow. Stir occasionally.

After initial aging, strain liqueur through metal colander placed over a large bowl. Press juice out of rhubarb with spoon. Discard rhubarb. Strain again through cloth until clear. Re-bottle as desired, cap and age at least 1 additional month before serving.

TABOO LIQUEUR

This wonderful liqueur made from a mixture of fresh citrus fruits is reminiscent of the famous **Forbidden Fruits Liqueur®**. *Our taste-test panel said this was one of the most exquisite tasting liqueurs they had sampled. Ready in 1 month, but improves with additional time. Makes over 1 quart.*

thin peel from 1 orange, chopped
thin peel from 1 lemon, chopped
1 cup freshly squeezed grapefruit juice (about 2 grapefruits)
1 cup freshly squeezed orange juice (2 to 3 oranges)
¼ cup freshly squeezed lemon juice (1 lemon)
2¼ cups granulated cane sugar
4-inch piece of vanilla bean, split lengthwise
1 cup brandy
1 cup vodka

In a medium saucepan, combine peels, grapefruit, orange and lemon juice, sugar and vanilla bean. Bring to a boil. Reduce heat; simmer, stirring frequently for 10 to 12 minutes. Cool to lukewarm.

Pour cooled mixture into aging container; add brandy and vodka. Allow liqueur to age for 3 weeks, then strain several times using successively finer strainers, or fine cloth. For maximum clarity, let liqueur stand for several days between strainings. Pour liqueur into bottles and cap.

VARIATION:

Honey may be substituted for all or part of the sugar. American whiskey may be substituted for the brandy.

STRAWBERRY LIQUEUR I

On these pages, you'll find two versions of **Liqueur des Fraises,** *a traditional liqueur that heralds the summer season. Pick fresh strawberries for this delicate liqueur. For the best flavor use only fresh berries and prepare while at their peak of freshness. Ready in 3½ months. Makes about 1 fifth.*

   3 cups fresh strawberries
   ½ cup powdered sugar
   2 cups vodka
   ½ cup granulated cane sugar
   2 tablespoons water
   2 tablespoons glycerin

Wash and stem berries. Pat dry. Cut berries in half and place in aging container. Cover berries with powdered sugar. Pour vodka over sugared berries. Stir just to combine. Cap container and let age in a cool, dark place for 2 to 3 weeks.

After initial aging period, combine granulated sugar and water in small saucepan.* Heat and stir until sugar is well dissolved. Set aside to cool.

Strain berry liquid through wire-mesh strainer placed over large bowl. With the back of a wooden spoon crush out liqueur liquid caught in berries. Discard berry pulp. Re-strain mixture through cloth to further remove sediment. Add cooled sugar-water mixture to strained strawberry liqueur. Stir to combine. Add glycerin and bottle as desired. Age at least 1 month before serving.

   *MICROWAVE DIRECTIONS: Combine granulated sugar and water in a glass 1-cup measure, stir. Microwave on HIGH power for 30 seconds. Stir to dissolve all sugar. Set aside to cool. Follow remaining directions.

STRAWBERRY LIQUEUR II

*Another version of **Liqueur des Fraises**, this is a larger, but easy, recipe to catch the fleeting fresh strawberry season. Use sweet, ripe berries but be careful to avoid over-ripe and/or moldy berries. Ready in 2 months. Makes about 1½ quarts.*

1¼ cups granulated cane sugar
1 fifth (750 ml) vodka
4 cups sliced fresh strawberries
2 tablespoons glycerin

In large aging container (or divide into two), combine sugar and vodka. Stir well to partly dissolve. Add strawberries, stir. Cap container. Stir or shake container daily for 2 weeks, or until sugar is completely dissolved.

When sugar is dissolved, place in cool, dark place for 6 weeks. Strain off strawberries after second aging. Discard berry pulp. Re-strain through fine muslin or coffee filters for clarity. Add glycerin and bottle as desired.

VARIATION:

WILD STRAWBERRY LIQUEUR is made with the same recipe. Wild strawberries are sometimes more tart and usually smaller. Sweetness may be increased, if desired, but often the refreshing tartness of the wild strawberries is enjoyed by following the recipe exactly.

PICANTE PEPPER LIQUEUR

If you're a fan of red pepper jelly, you may find you develop a serious infatuation with **Picante Pepper Liqueur.** *Our basic recipe is peppery but tame, with a zesty variation, depending upon the peppers used. See the suggestions below to vary the heat. A wonderful choice served with cheese. Makes just under one quart.*

1½ pounds peppers (see suggestions below)*
2 cups granulated cane sugar
2¾ cups vodka
¾ cup brandy

Wash peppers and pat dry. Cut each into decorative strips and discard seed. Place in a large aging container. Add sugar, vodka and brandy to plums; stir to combine. Cover, let age 3 to 4 months in a cool, dark place; stir monthly.

After initial aging, strain mixture through wire-mesh strainer over large mixing bowl. Press out liqueur in peppers with back of a wooden spoon. (Save pepper strips for use in cooking. Delicious chopped in cornbread batter.) Re-strain through cloth until clear. Bottle as desired. Age for additional 1 month. Liqueur is ready to serve.

* For a mild pepper taste, use equal numbers of large bell peppers and jalapeños, to a weight of 1½ pounds.

VARIATION:

ZESTY PEPPER LIQUEUR, substitute one or two hotter peppers, such as serrano or habañero for some or all of the jalapeños.

PRICKLY PEAR LIQUEUR

You have probably seen large Prickly Pear Cactus loaded with large fruit, called pears, growing in the desert states of the United States and in Mexico. It also grows in southern Italy where it is known as liquore di fico d'indica or in Sardinia where it is known as liquore figu morisca. In these areas you can find the prickly pear cactus locally; however, we are now seeing it in a number of produce markets.

It is an exotic and interesting fruit liqueur and the color is gorgeous, a lovely magenta tint. Here is a recipe so you can try this unique fruit liqueur. The Sardinian version adds lemon zest otherwise the recipes are very similiar. Make sure you use good tasting water, purified or distilled is good. Water with chlorine does not belong in any liqueur. Yields: 1 quart

10 whole prickly pears, handle carefully due to the needles
4 strips of lemon zest, optional
1 pint 80- or 100-proof vodka
1⅔ cups (14 ounces) water
1⅔ cups (14 ounces) granulated cane sugar

Carefully remove needles and peel cactus pears.

Steep cactus fruit and lemon zest if using, in alcohol for 2 weeks. The alcohol aquires a dark orange to red color from the fruit.

Make a syrup heating the water and sugar in a medium saucepan. Stir until dissolved and slightly thickened. Cool and set aside.

Remove fruit, strain and add the sugar syrup. Re-strain if necessary and age in a cool, dark place for 30 days. Bottle as desired.

Making Non-Fruit Liqueurs

ADVOCAAT

*Our version of Dutch **Advocaat** and **Eggnog Liqueur** takes its name from the Dutch word for 'lawyer.' Advocaat is a traditonal European liqueur. Mild, velvety, with a hint of lemon, it's quickly made at any time of year, but is especially popular during the holiday season as a refreshing alternative to eggnog. Ready in 2 to 3 weeks, Makes about 1½ quarts.*

    1¼ cups granulated cane sugar
    ¾ teaspoon vanilla
    ½ teaspoon lemon extract
    1 cup vodka
    5 whole eggs*
    1 egg yolk*
    ⅔ cup evaporated milk

(Directions given are for blender or food processor preparation. Can be made in a bowl if beaten well.)

Put sugar into blender or food processor with steel knife, blend. Add remaining ingredients and combine for 30 seconds or until mixed well. Pour into container/bottles, cap and refrigerate.

Age for 1 to 2 weeks to mellow. Color will intensify as it ages, reaching a more traditional light shade of yellow. Keep refrigerated.

*NOTE Although this recipe is traditionally made with ordinary raw eggs, it's now known that raw eggs can harbor the bacteria salmonella. A safer approach is to use "pasteurized" eggs, which are available at many supermarkets. They may be used successfully in this recipe.

Pasteurized eggs look just like ordinary eggs; however, they've been heated slightly to kill any salmonella bacteria. (This is not a process that can be duplicated in the home kitchen.) And always, when using eggs, we suggest basic precautions: start with clean, uncracked eggs and be sure to keep this liqueur refrigerated.

Amaretto Liqueur

*Our liqueur will remind you of the famous, oldest and best-known almond liqueur in the world today, **Amaretto di Saronno**®, a liqueur that has been made in Italy since the fifteenth century. Ours is ready in just 1 to 2 months. Makes over 1 fifth.*

> ½ pound (2 cups) sliced, chopped or slivered almonds
> 3 cups brandy
> ½ cup vodka
> 1 tablespoon orange rind *
> 4 dried apricot halves. chopped
> 1¼ cups granulated cane sugar
> ½ cup water
> 2 teaspoons almond extract
> 2 tablespoons glycerin

Place almonds in an aging container. Add brandy, vodka, orange rind and apricots. Stir, cap and age for 1 to 2 months in a cool, dark place. Stir and test almond flavor after 1 month to determine if additional aging is desired; for a more pronounced flavor, age for a second month.

After initial aging, strain clear liqueur liquid through colander or wire-mesh strainer into a bowl. Re-strain through a cloth bag to remove fine particles. (Almonds and dried apricots may be saved for cooking.)

Combine sugar and ½ cup water in a small saucepan. Bring to boil, stirring constantly. Reduce heat and simmer until all sugar is dissolved. Remove from heat and let cool. Add cooled sugar-water, almond extract, and glycerin to aged liqueur. Rebottle as desired. Liqueur is ready to serve, but will continue to improve with additional aging.

* Include some of the bitter white part of the orange rind when peeling orange.

ANGELICA LIQUEUR

A flavorful liqueur using the herb angelica came from friend and noted herb expert, Terry Tucker Francis. Angelica (Angelica archangelica) has a long history in Europe for use in food, medicine and fragrance. Its essential oils flavor famous liqueurs, such as Benedictine®, Chartreuse®, Ratafia d'Angelique and Vermouth. Dried angelica root is available at health food and herb stores. Ready in 1½ months. Makes about 1 pint.

3 tablespoons dried chopped angelica root
1 tablespoon chopped almonds
1 allspice berry, cracked
1-inch piece of cinnamon stick, broken
3 to 6 anise or fennel seeds, crushed
⅛ teaspoon powdered coriander seed
1 tablespoon chopped fresh **or** 1 teaspoon dried marjoram leaves
1½ cups vodka
½ cup granulated cane sugar
¼ cup water
1 drop each yellow and green food coloring (optional)

Combine all herbs, nuts and spices with vodka in 1-quart or larger aging container. Cap tightly and shake daily for 2 weeks. Strain through fine muslin cloth or coffee filter paper, discarding solids. Clean out aging container. Place strained liqueur liquid into clean aging container.

Place sugar and water in saucepan* and stir to combine over medium heat. When sugar is completely dissolved, set aside and let cool. When cool, combine with food coloring and add to liqueur liquid. Cap and allow to age and mellow in a cool, dark place for 1 month.

*MICROWAVE DIRECTIONS: To do this step in a microwave oven use a glass bowl. Microwave on HIGH (100%) for 1 to 1½ minutes, stirring every 30 seconds.

ANISETTE

Italian Anisette is an anise-flavored liqueur that is sweeter and gentler than the Greek Ouzo. Delightful in our buttery **Italian Änise Star Cookies.** *Ready in 3 months. Makes about 1 quart.*

> 1 teaspoon coriander seeds
> 5 teaspoons anise extract
> 1 fifth vodka
> 2 cups light corn syrup

Crush coriander seeds in a mortar or small bowl, using pestle or back of spoon. Place in aging container and add other ingredients. Cap and shake or stir well to combine. Let stand in a cool, dark place for 1 month, shaking every few days.

After initial aging, strain liqueur through a fine cloth bag placed in wiremesh strainer, over a large bowl. Bottle and age an additional 2 months.

AQUAVIT

A Scandinavian drink that is traditionally served ice-cold in small glasses. Serve with cheeses, seafood or smorgasbord. Often chased with a golden beer. Best made with a high quality vodka. Ready in 3 weeks. Makes 1 fifth.

> 1 tablespoon caraway seeds*
> 1 fifth vodka

Bruise caraway seeds by crushing with pestle or back of spoon in mortar or bowl. Add to vodka. Cap and let stand in cool, dark place for 3 weeks. Strain off seeds. Re-strain for clarity.

*Additional spices such as cardamom or anise may be added as desired.

OUZO LIQUEUR

*No fence-sitter here! Greek **Ouzo**'s certainly not a middle-of-the-road liqueur. Its powerful taste and kick will delight some and chase away quite a few. In other words, you'll love it or hate it. But wait—don't dismiss it so quickly. Used in cooking, for its unique anise flavor, Ouzo is a winner! You'll love it in our **International Cheese Soup** recipe. Ready in 3 months. Makes about 1 fifth.*

½ cup boiling water
4 teaspoons granulated cane sugar
¼ teaspoon dried angelica root, chopped
pinch of mace
4 teaspoons anise extract
1½ cups pure grain alcohol
¾ to 1 cup water*

Combine boiling water and sugar in the aging container; stir or shake until sugar is dissolved. Stir in dried angelica root and mace. Cool to lukewarm, then add anise extract, pure grain alcohol and water. Shake to combine. Cover and let stand for 3 days. Strain and re-bottle. Allow this liqueur to age for 1 month.

*You may adjust the alcohol strength to your taste by adjusting the quantity of water as shown and still have an authentic Ouzo.

KÜMMEL LIQUEUR

Caraway seeds, which are actually the dried fruit of the **carum carvi** *plant, are the predominant flavoring in this traditional Old World liqueur. The versatile* **Kümmel** *will become a favorite before-dinner aperitif or an after-dinner refresher, as well as a unique ingredient in many drinks. Used in cooking, it will enliven your breads, vegetables, sausages and pork dishes with its warm, aromatic goodness. Ready in to 2 months. Makes just over 1 fifth.*

    2½ tablespoons caraway seeds
    ¼ teaspoon fennel seeds
    2 whole cloves
    3 cups vodka*
    ⅔ cup granulated cane sugar
    ½ cup water

Bruise caraway and fennel seeds with pestle or the back of a wooden spoon.

Place in aging container with whole cloves. Stir in vodka or pure grain alcohol and water. Cap and let stand 24 hours. Remove cloves, re-cap and let age 2 to 3 more weeks in a cool, dark place. Shake occasionally.

After initial aging, strain off seeds. Combine sugar and water in a saucepan and heat to a boil, stirring to dissolve sugar. Remove from heat and let cool. Add cooled sugar syrup to liqueur; stir. Cap and age 1 to 2 months more.

Re-strain, if necessary, to make liqueur particle-free. Re-bottle as desired.

* 1½ cups pure grain alcohol and 1½ cups water may be substituted for the 3 cups vodka in this recipe.

CARAWAY LIQUEUR

Slightly sweeter than **Kümmel**, *this liqueur is made in the Scandinavian tradition. Ready in 1 to 2 months. Makes about 1 quart.*

2 tablespoons caraway seeds, crushed*
1 tablespoon fennel seeds, crushed
1 teaspoon coriander seeds
3 cups vodka
1½ to 2 cups granulated cane sugar
¾ cup distilled water

Combine spices with alcohol in a 1-quart or larger aging container. Cover and let stand for 7 to 14 days in a cool place.

After initial aging, add sugar and water by the following method. Bring water to a boil and pour over sugar. Stir to dissolve completely and let cool. Strain off seeds by pouring through a mesh strainer into a bowl. Re-strain through a finer strainer as necessary to remove all seed material. Then combine cool sugar mixture and liqueur into a clean aging container. Age in a cool, dark place for 3 to 4 weeks. Bottle as desired.

*Your choice of spices may be used in this liqueur. With caraway seeds as the base ingredient, add fennel seeds, coriander seeds, juniper berries or other herbs, spices or seeds to your taste. Follow the general proportions in **Caraway Liqueur** recipe.

CRÈME DE MENTHE LIQUEUR

This traditional **Crème de Menthe Liqueur** *uses extract rather than fresh mint as in the* **Fresh Mint Liqueur**. *It can be made in the three commercial shades of clear, gold and green. Ready in 1 month. Makes approximately 1¼ quarts.*

> 4 cups granulated cane sugar
> 2 cups water
> 3 cups vodka
> 1 tablespoon mint or peppermint extract
> 2 tablespoons glycerin

In saucepan, combine sugar and water. Bring to a boil, stirring constantly. When sugar is dissolved, set aside to cool. In aging container, combine remaining ingredients. Add cooled sugar syrup, stirring to combine. Re-bottle now or after initial 1 month aging.

VARIATIONS:

GOLD CRÈME DE MENTHE is made by adding yellow food coloring, a touch of red, and the merest hint of blue, by drops, to the basic clear recipe until desired color is achieved. (We suggest that you practice with food coloring and water first!) Age as directed.

GREEN CRÈME DE MENTHE – Add green and blue food coloring, by drops, until desired color is reached. Age as directed.

FRESH MINT LIQUEUR

*In our search for natural-based liqueurs, we automatically turned to our home-grown mint beds to reproduce **Crème de Menthe Liqueur**. What we achieved was a fresher, milder, more delicate liqueur that is in many ways superior to the classic. You may wish to try both recipes to discover your own preference. Ready in 1½ to 3 months. Makes approximately 1 quart.*

    1½ cups fresh mint leaves, slightly packed
    3 cups vodka
    2 cups granulated cane sugar
    1 cup water
    1 tablespoon glycerin
    8 drops green food coloring
    2 drops blue food coloring

Wash mint leaves in cold water several times. Shake or pat dry gently. Snip each leaf in half or thirds; discard stems. Measure cut mint leaves, packing slightly. Combine mint leaves and vodka in aging container. Cap and let stand in a cool place for 2 weeks, shaking occasionally.

After initial aging, pour liqueur through colander into a large bowl to remove leaves; discard leaves. Re-strain through finer mesh as needed for clarity.

In saucepan, combine sugar and water. Bring to a boil, stirring constantly. Let cool. Add cooled sugar syrup to mint liqueur base, stirring to combine. Add glycerin and food color; pour into aging container for secondary aging of 1 to 3 more months.

VARIATION:

FRESH CRÈME DE MENTHE - if you like a slightly heavier emphasis on the mint, adjust to taste by adding drops of mint extract (up to 1 teaspoon) to Fresh Mint Liqueur.

MEXICAN COFFEE LIQUEUR

*Introducing our version of **Kahlúa**®! No book on liqueur making would be complete without a coffee liqueur recipe similar to Kahlua®. Research was no problem, since almost everyone gave us their "Kahlua®" recipe. We hoped one of them would be perfect. However, this turned out to be one of the more difficult liqueurs to simulate accurately. Not one of the recipes came close—and some of these are even in print! Kahlua® is a complex liqueur and requires a more complex list of ingredients than brown sugar and vodka. Try this recipe and we think you'll agree it bears an accurate resemblance to classic Kahlua®. Ready in 2 to 4 months. Makes about 1½ quarts.*

> 2 cups water
> ¼ cup plus 2 teaspoons instant coffee granules or powder*
> 3½ cups granulated cane sugar
> 1 vanilla bean, split lengthwise
> 2¾ cups vodka
> ¾ cup brandy
> ¼ teaspoon chocolate extract
> 1 drop red food coloring

Heat water in medium saucepan. When hot, add coffee and stir until dissolved. Add sugar and vanilla bean, stirring well to combine. Bring to a boil, stirring constantly. Immediately reduce heat so that a very low boil is maintained for 1 minute. Remove from heat and cool to lukewarm. Pour vodka and brandy into aging container. Add the cooled coffee mixture and the chocolate extract. Stir well. Cap and let age in a cool, dark place for 3 weeks.

After initial aging, strain liqueur through a cloth-lined wire-mesh strainer over a large bowl. Save vanilla bean for another use. Repeat until desired clarity is reached. Stir in food coloring. Bottle, cap and let age an additional 1 to 3 months.

*For best results use a freshly opened jar of coffee.

OLD JAMAICA COFFEE LIQUEUR

*There are many well-known coffee liqueurs, but one of the most popular is the Jamaican **Tia Maria**®. Our rum-based recipe is similar to this famous liqueur. Naturally, the taste will vary depending upon the types of rum and coffee used. For authenticity, use Jamaican light rum and a premium quality instant coffee. Ready in 2 to 3 months. Makes approximately 1½ quarts.*

> 2½ cups water
> ¼ cup instant coffee granules or powder*
> 2 cups granulated cane sugar
> 1 vanilla bean, split lengthwise
> 1 fifth light rum
> 1½ teaspoons glycerin, optional

Heat water in a medium saucepan. When hot, stir in coffee until dissolved. Add sugar and vanilla bean, stirring to combine. Bring to a boil, lower heat and simmer for one minute, stirring constantly. Remove from heat; cool to lukewarm.

When cool, add rum; stir well. Pour into aging container; cover tightly and allow the liqueur to age 3 weeks in a cool, dark place.

After initial aging, strain liqueur through a cloth-lined wire-mesh strainer over a large bowl. Save vanilla bean for another use. Add glycerin, re-bottle, and age an additional 1 to 3 months.

* A freshly opened jar of instant coffee will give the best results.

NASSAU VANILLA LIQUEUR

*Our Nassau Vanilla Liqueur is similar to the well-known **Nassau Royale**®. This liqueur, with its rich vanilla complemented by dark rum, may be served at room temperature or slightly warm, in the tradition of Amaretto Liqueur or a fine brandy. Ready in 2 to 3 months. Makes just under 1 quart.*

  2½ cups dark rum
  4 vanilla beans, split lengthwise**
  1 cup granulated cane sugar
  1 cup water
  2 tablespoons glycerin

Combine rum and vanilla beans in aging container. Cap and shake to mix. Age in a cool, dark place for 2 to 3 weeks.

In a small saucepan combine sugar and water* Stir over medium heat until mixture comes to a boil. Remove from heat; continue stirring until all sugar is dissolved. Let cool.

Strain aged rum and vanilla bean mixture by pouring through coffee filter or cloth bag placed in strainer over medium bowl. Save vanilla beans.**

Combine cooled sugar syrup with liqueur. Stir in glycerin. Bottle, cap and age an additional 1 to 2 months before serving.

*MICROWAVE DIRECTIONS: Combine sugar and water in a 2-cup glass measure. Microwave on HIGH (100%) power for 30 seconds. Stir with wooden spoon. Microwave for 30 to 45 seconds more. Remove from microwave and stir until all sugar is dissolved. Let cool and proceed as directed.

**Our Vanilla Sugar recipe on page 163 is a great way to recycle vanilla beans used in liqueur making.

H & C'S IRISH CREAM LIQUEUR

In our testing for an Irish Cream Liqueur, we used, as our standard, Bailey's Original Irish Cream®—so good and so expensive! We found this one of the most difficult liqueurs to reproduce. We tried lots of "homemade" recipes, but all missed the mark of our standard: the best. So we threw everything out (except the Bailey's) and started again. Relax; we finally got it just right, inexpensive, quick and easy! Ready in just 1 week. Serve within 6 months. Makes approximately 1 fifth.

2 large eggs*
1⅓ cups evaporated milk
½ teaspoon chocolate syrup
1 tablespoon pure vanilla extract
⅓ teaspoon lemon extract
¼ teaspoon instant coffee
¾ cup granulated cane sugar
1¾ cups Irish whiskey

Place all ingredients in blender; blend well. Bottle and let mellow in refrigerator at least one week before serving. We found this best after 1 to 2 weeks. Store in refrigerator.

*NOTE: Although this recipe is traditionally made with ordinary raw eggs, it's now known that raw eggs can harbor the bacteria salmonella. This problem is more prevalent in certain parts of the country. A safer approach is to use "pasteurized eggs," which are available at many supermarkets. They may be used successfully in this recipe.

Pasteurized eggs look just like ordinary eggs, however they've been heated slightly to kill any possible salmonella. (This is not a process that can be duplicated in the home kitchen.) As always, when using any eggs, We suggest basic precautions: start with clean, uncracked eggs and be sure to keep this liqueur refrigerated.

ITALIANO GOLD LIQUEUR

This is our version of **Liquore Galliano®**, *that brilliant yellow liqueur in the tall, skinny bottle. It's a popular challenge to the "at-home" liqueur maker and is one of the most difficult to copy precisely. We tested countless recipes that didn't come close to the original, before developing a quality liqueur of sufficient complexity that did.*

Almost without exception, every homemade recipe we found used 80-proof vodka. However, in our search for authentic flavor, we found that a stronger base was mandatory. Therefore, we used pure grain alcohol and we suggest that you follow our guidelines. 100-proof vodka, where available, would be an adequate substitute (see note). Ready in 3 to 6 months. Makes approximately 1 quart.

    1 teaspoon chopped, dried angelica root
    3-inch cinnamon stick
    1 whole clove
    1 pinch nutmeg
    1 vanilla bean, split lengthwise
    2½ cups water*
    2 cups granulated cane sugar
    1 tablespoon lemon juice
    ½ teaspoon anìse extract
    ½ teaspoon banana extract
    ½ teaspoon (scant) pineapple extract
    1½ cups pure grain alcohol*
    1 tablespoon glycerin
    2 to 3 drops yellow food coloring

Line a wire-mesh strainer with a paper coffee filter. Set strainer over a one-quart mixing bowl. Place dried angelica root, cinnamon, clove, nutmeg and vanilla bean in a medium saucepan. Add water; heat until mixture comes to a boil. Remove from heat. Let stand 15 seconds, then pour through the prepared strainer into the bowl. (It is important to work quickly or spices

will impart too strong a color and taste to the liquid.) Reserve the vanilla bean; discard the other spices.

Rinse the saucepan and pour the liquid back into it. Add the reserved vanilla bean and the sugar. Heat until mixture comes to a boil; reduce heat and simmer 1 minute, stirring constantly. Remove from heat and cool to room temperature.

When cool, add the lemon juice, extracts, and alcohol, stirring to combine. Pour into aging container. Cap and let age in a cool, dark place for 1 week.

After initial aging, strain through a cloth bag set in a wire-mesh strainer over a large bowl. Repeat until desired clarity is reached. Stir in glycerin and food coloring. Bottle, seal and age for 3 to 6 months.

*If substituting 100-proof vodka for the alcohol, use 3 cups of vodka and reduce the water to 1 cup.

ITALIAN HERB LIQUEUR

The noted Italian herbal liqueur, Strega®, is made with over seventy herbs. It was used as a bewitching love potion in days gone by, perhaps because of its name, which means, "witch." In fact, this liqueur is often popularly known as The Witch. We hope you love our simplified recipe. Ready in 2 months. Makes about 1 quart.

> 6 cardamom pods
> 1 tablespoon star anise or anise seed
> 1 tablespoon chopped, dried angelica root
> 3-inch cinnamon stick
> 2 cloves
> ¼ teaspoon mace
> 1 fifth vodka
> 1 cup honey

In small mortar, crush cardamom seeds (which have been removed from pods). Add star anise and break up slightly. Place into 1½-quart or larger aging container. Add remainder of herbs. Stir in vodka. Cap and let age in a cool, dark place for 1 week.

After initial aging, strain off all seeds through metal strainer. Re-strain through coffee filter or muslin cloth bag to remove tiny particles. Wash and dry aging container. Pour clear herbal liquid back into aging container. Stir in the honey. Cap and age in a cool, dark place for 8 weeks.

Do not move or stir this liqueur during the second aging; this will allow the cloudiness from the honey to settle. Siphon off the clear liqueur. See Siphoning directions on page 15. Bottle as desired.

HAZELNUT LIQUEUR

Oregon hazelnuts are a key ingredient in this "taste-alike" version of the delicate Italian **Frangelico® Liqueur**. Ready in 6 months. Makes about 1 quart.

> 4 cups (about 1 pound) unshelled hazelnuts (filberts)
> 1 teaspoon chopped dried angelica root
> ½ vanilla bean, split lengthwise
> 1 fifth vodka
> ¼ teaspoon almond extract
> 1½ cups granulated cane sugar
> 1 cup water
> 2 tablespoons glycerin
> 1 to 2 drops yellow food coloring (optional, to correct color if necessary)

Preheat oven to 350°F. Shell hazelnuts. Coarsely chop hazelnuts and place on a baking sheet in the oven for 10 to 15 minutes. Remove from oven, cool, and place in an aging container. Stir in dried angelica root, vanilla bean, vodka and almond extract. Cap and let age for 1 month in a cool, dark place, shaking occasionally.

After aging, pour through fine mesh strainer into a large bowl. Rinse out aging container. Place cloth bag or triple cheesecloth inside a large funnel. Place funnel over aging container and pour liqueur through.

In medium saucepan, combine sugar and water; bring to a boil. Immediately reduce heat and simmer for a few minutes, stirring to dissolve sugar completely. Let cool. When sugar syrup has cooled, add to aging container, stirring well to combine. Cap and let age 3 months.

After second aging, re-strain through cloth or paper coffee filters until desired clarity is reached. Stir in glycerin and food coloring, if desired. Let age 2 more months before serving.

SCOTTISH HIGHLAND LIQUEUR

The well-known and well-loved **Drambuie**® *is a Scottish tradition. As the legend is told, this herbal liqueur was once a favorite of Bonnie Prince Charlie, who in 1746 gave his secret recipe to the Mackinnons of Strathaird in gratitude for their shelter and assistance after his army was defeated. The name Drambuie*® *is derived from the Gaelic words "an dram buidbeach" which mean, "the drink that satisfies." That phrase applies as well to* **Scottish Highland Liqueur,** *our version of Drambuie*®. *One sip and you're sure to hear the bagpipes! Ready in 6½ months. Makes 1 quart.*

> 1 fifth Johnny Walker Black Label Scotch® *
> 1½ cups mild honey
> 2 teaspoons dried, chopped angelica root
> ¼ teaspoon fennel seeds, crushed
> two 2-inch strips lemon zest

Combine all ingredients in aging container. Cover tightly and shake gently several times during the first 24 hours. After 24 hours, remove the lemon zest. Cover again and let stand in a cool, dark place for 2 weeks, shaking or stirring gently every other day.

Strain through a wire sieve to remove the angelica root and fennel. Return to aging container; cover and let stand undisturbed in a cool, dark place for 6 months. Siphon or pour clear liqueur into a sterile bottle. The cloudy dregs may be saved for cooking.

*We are *very fussy* about the Scotch in this recipe! For best results use the recommended brand.

Making Infused Brandy Liqueurs

Brandies have always been a fascination. Not only are they flavorful in their own right, but they lend a richness to liqueurs that is incomparable. Somewhere in the middle, between brandy in its natural state and a liqueur are the **Infused Brandies,** and these along with **Infused Brandy Liqueurs,** are both delightful additions to this book.

A Word About Brandy

As we've mentioned earlier, basic brandy is distilled from fermented grape juices, although you'll find that some brandies are made from other fruits, such as apple and pear. The wide range of brandies available on the market can be confusing, so sampling different brands is a very good idea.

Generally, the rule of thumb is that for liqueurs that use brandy only as an enhancement to the dominant flavor of the fruit or spices a less-costly brandy is quite acceptable. But as the percentage of brandy in the recipe increases, the quality of the brandy becomes more important and you will want to use a brandy with a flavor you appreciate.

However, any of these recipes can be made with a reasonably priced brandy that does not require a large investment.

Do stay away from "fruit-flavored brandies" in your liqueur-making, to allow the essence of the recipe's ingredients to make their own statement.

The Art of Infused Brandies

To be perfectly correct, all of the liqueurs in this book are "infused"— that is, they are made by aging flavors and sweeteners, so that when the fruit, or spice is later removed, its flavor has been infused in the alcohol base.

What makes this chapter different is that the primary alcohol base is brandy or cognac. If you haven't yet explored brandy's possibilities, these recipes should get you started toward very tasty sipping!

ADVOCAAT BRANDY

*Here's the Dutch Lawyer's Liqueur for brandy-lovers. Both this version , and the traditional **Advocaat** on page 59, are our favorite winter holiday liqueurs. Better than eggnog any day! Ready in 2 to 3 weeks, Makes about 1½ quarts.*

1¼ cups granulated cane sugar
¾ teaspoon vanilla
½ teaspoon lemon extract
½ cup brandy
½ cup vodka
5 whole eggs*
1 egg yolk*
⅔ cup evaporated milk

(Directions given are for blender or food processor preparation. Can be made in a bowl if beaten well.)

Put sugar into blender or food processor with steel knife, blend. Add remaining ingredients and combine for 30 seconds or until well mixed. Pour into container/bottles, cap and refrigerate.

Age for 1 to 2 weeks to mellow. Color will intensify as it ages, reaching a more traditional light shade of yellow. Keep refrigerated.

*NOTE Although this recipe is traditionally made with ordinary raw eggs, it's now known that raw eggs can harbor the bacteria salmonella. A safer approach is to use "pasteurized" eggs, which are available at many supermarkets. They may be used successfully in this recipe.

Pasteurized eggs look just like ordinary eggs; however, they've been heated slightly to kill any salmonella bacteria. (This is not a process that can be duplicated in the home kitchen.) And always, when using eggs, we suggest basic precautions: start with clean, uncracked eggs and be sure to keep this liqueur refrigerated.

BRANDIED APPLE LIQUEUR

Brandied Apple Liqueur, our version of the famous liqueur, Calvados, can easily be made in the home kitchen. Because the cognac plays a dominant role, it is necessary to use a good quality brand with a flavor you enjoy. Ready in 2 to 3 months. Makes over 1 quart.

2½ pounds sweet apples*
1 cup vodka
3 cups quality French cognac
1½ cups granulated cane sugar
¾ cup water

Wash apples and remove stems. Cut into wedges or slices and put into aging container. Pour vodka and brandy over apples, stirring with a wooden spoon. Cap and age in a cool place for 1 month.

Pour liqueur mixture through a fine cloth bag that has been placed into a large bowl. Set bag with apples into another bowl to drain. Clean aging container, removing any sediment. Pour strained liqueur back into clean aging container. Twist top of bag and with the back of a spoon press out any liqueur possible. (Some apples are soft and easy to press, others are hard and don't permit much liquid to be pressed out.) Pour liqueur/juice into aging container.

Combine sugar and water in a small saucepan. Heat, bringing up to a boil, stir constantly. Set aside to cool. Pour strained liqueur and cooled sugar-water into aging container. Cap container and let age at least 1 more month. This liqueur improves with additional aging, so an additional month beyond this time produces an even finer product.

After aging time, check clarity. If any additional straining is needed, do it this time. A fine wire mesh, cloth or coffee filter is best for finer straining. When desired clarity is reached, bottle and store in a cool, dark place.

PEACH INFUSED BRANDY

Our version of the popular Southern Comfort. Use fresh peaches, any variety. Save the peaches after straining and serve over ice cream. Top a peach pie with whipped cream and liqueured peaches—wow! Ready in just over 1 month. Makes about 1 fifth.

1½ pounds peaches
1 cup granulated cane sugar
4 strips lemon peel
2 cups bourbon or brandy

Peel, pit, and slice peaches. Place in saucepan.* Add sugar, stir well to cornbine. Warm over low heat until sugar is well dissolved and peaches are juicy.

Place peach mixture into aging container. Add lemon peels and bourbon, stirring to combine. Cover container and put in a cool, dark place, or refrigerate if necessary. Let stand for 1 week, stirring occasionally.

After 1 week aging, strain liqueur mixture through medium wire strainer placed over a large mixing bowl. Press out liqueur liquid in peaches by pressing with the back of a wooden spoon. Either discard peach pulp or save for use in other recipes.

Re-strain through finer wire-mesh or cloth until desired clarity is reached. Bottle as desired. Liqueur is fine for cooking at this point and is drinkable. Improves with additional aging.

*MICROWAVE DIRECTIONS: Place peaches and sugar into large microwave-safe mixing bowl. Stir to combine. Microwave on HIGH (100%) power for 6 to 7 minutes, stirring every 2 minutes. Proceed as directed.

RASPBERRY BRANDY LIQUEUR

A magnificent infused brandy liqueur that embraces the rich color and flavor of fresh raspberries. Ready in 1 month. Makes about 1½ quarts.

4 cups raspberries
1 pint water
granulated cane sugar* (see note below)
1 3-inch strip lemon zest
1 pint quality unflavored brandy

Rinse and sort berries in cool water, removing any over-ripe or moldy ones. Put berries and water into a large enamel pot. Heat, stirring occasionally, until mixture reaches a boil. Reduce heat to maintain a low simmer for 12 minutes or until berries lose their shape, stirring every few minutes. Strain mixture through a fine wire mesh sieve, discarding berry pulp. Measure strained berry liquid and set aside. Clean the pot, then pour berry liquid back into it.

Stir sugar and lemon zest into berry liquid. Heat, stirring often until mixture comes to a boil. Reduce heat to a simmer and maintain for 12 minutes. Let cool, then strain through a cloth.

Add brandy to cooled mixture; stir to combine. When completely cooled, bottle as desired, cap and age in a cool, dark place for 4 weeks.

*NOTE: Sugar amount will vary, depending upon the amount of berry liquid obtained. Use ¾ cup granulated cane sugar per pint of berry liquid.

SPICED BLACKBERRY BRANDY LIQUEUR

A wonderfully rich infused brandy liqueur that can be made with a variety of cane berries. Our favorites are Blackberries, wild or cultivated; Marionberries or plump Boysenberries. A sip of this in the winter is summer remembered. Makes an especially lovely gift. Ready in 1 month. Makes about 1½ quarts.

    8 cups blackberries
    1 pint water
    granulated cane sugar* (see note below)
    spices of choice (some or all):
        ¼ teaspoon whole cloves
        ¼ teaspoon whole allspice
        1 4-inch cinnamon stick
        1 whole nutmeg, cracked
    1 pint quality unflavored brandy

Rinse and sort berries in cool water, removing any over-ripe or moldy ones. Put berries and water into a large enamel pot. Heat, stirring occasionally, until mixture reaches a boil. Reduce heat to maintain a low simmer for 12 minutes or until berries lose their shape, stirring every few minutes. Strain mixture, discarding berry pulp. Measure strained berry liquid and set aside. Clean the pot, then pour berry liquid back into it.

*NOTE: Sugar amount will vary, depending upon the amount of berry liquid obtained. Use ¾ cup granulated cane sugar per pint of berry liquid.

Stir sugar into berry liquid. Select some or all of the spices and put into a spice bag, or tie in a bundle of a double-layer of cheesecloth. Add spice bag to the berry liquid, then heat, stirring often until mixture comes to a boil. Reduce heat to a simmer and maintain for 12 minutes. Remove spice bag and let cool.

Add brandy to cooled mixture; stir to combine. When completely cooled, bottle as desired, cap and age in a cool, dark place for 4 weeks.

LEMON GINGER INFUSED BRANDY

Lemon is a flavor we can never get enough of! Combined with an exotic hint of ginger, it produces an infused brandy that is fascinating. Makes about 3½ cups.

> 2 large lemons, sliced thin (Meyer lemons preferred)
> 4 ounces ginger root peeled cut into thin slices
> 1 vanilla bean, split lengthwise
> 1 cup granulated cane sugar
> water
> 3 cups brandy

Rinse lemon and pat dry. Thinly peel zest (thin outer layer) strips from lemon. Do not include whiter inner peel. Place zest strips, ginger root slices and vanilla bean into medium saucepan. Cut lemons in half and squeeze juice into measuring cup. Remove any seeds. Measure juice and add enough water to bring to the 1 cup mark. Pour lemon juice mixture into saucepan with zest, add sugar and stir. Bring mixture to a boil, stirring frequently. When it reaches a boil, reduce heat and simmer for 10 minutes. Remove from heat and cool.

Pour lemon-ginger mixture into aging container, add brandy and stir. Cap and age for 4 weeks in a cool, dark place.

After initial aging, pour through metal strainer into bowl to remove zest, ginger and vanilla bean. Pour liqueur back into cleaned aging container for an additional month of aging.

When aging is completed, strain liqueur through fine cloth (such as muslin) which is placed over a large bowl. Repeat as needed. The lemon may cause a cloudy layer to form on top even after several strainings. The cloudy portion may be poured off and reserved for cooking if desired. Bottle and cap as desired. Brandy is now ready to be used in cooking but is better for drinking after an additional 3 months' aging.

HIBISCUS BRANDY

A friend recently made a pure non-alcoholic hibiscus beverage that was absolutely delicious as well as being reputedly good for our health. With all that in mind, we turned to making an infused brandy from dried hibiscus flowers. We found its color and flavor beautiful. This is a small recipe and the aging is short, so a test batch is quick and easy. The recipe is easily doubled or made again for yourself or gifts. Good sources for the flowers are Mexican grocery stores, health food shops or online retailers. Make the simple syrup first. Yield: about 2 cups.

Simple syrup:
¼ cup granulated cane sugar
¼ cup water

Combine sugar and water in a small saucepan. Bring to a boil, stirring until all sugar has dissolved. Remove from heat. Set aside and let cool.

Hibiscus Brandy:
2 cups Brandy
¼ to ⅓ cup dried hibiscus flowers, to taste
1 thin strip of lemon zest, Meyer lemon preferred
After Initial Aging:
⅓ to ½ cup simple syrup, to taste*

Place dried hibiscus flowers and brandy in a glass quart jar or similar glass or ceramic container. Stir and cap—remember not to use metal or plastic containers. If the cap on your container place is metal, place a piece of plastic wrap under the cap, without it touching the brandy mixture.

Age in a cool, dark place for one week. Taste for depth of hibiscus flavor desired. Remove hibiscus flowers if strength is where you want it or leave in for another week's aging. If desired add lemon zest for second week. Taste after second week for depth of flavor. If the taste is to your liking, remove hibiscus flowers and lemon zest by straining into a bowl.

Wash aging container then pour strained mixture back into it. Next add simple syrup in the amount desired*.

Let age a week or two then pour into a glass decanter or bottle and cap. Enjoy this yourself or give as a gift.

*NOTE: If you are not sure of the sweetness you prefer, start with ⅓ cup and add more if desired.

FIGGY BRANDY

You can make this recipe with dried figs at any time of year. Very nice at a special meal or holiday.* This slightly sweet and fruity recipe makes an usual but memorable brandy for sipping or cooking. Makes about 1 quart.

10 ounces dried figs
1 cup (8 fl. oz) water
2 strips lemon zest, Meyer lemon preferred
¼ cup granulated cane sugar, to taste
1 qt. (32 fl. oz) brandy

Place dried figs, water and lemon zest into a saucepan. Bring just to a boil, lower heat, cover and simmer for 30 minutes, stirring occasionally. Remove from heat and let cool slightly. Pour cooled fig lemon mixture with syrup into a large aging jar or crock. Pour in brandy and stir gently to combine. Cap and place in a cool dark place for a month. Uncap and taste, age an additional month or two until flavor is right for you.

Strain out figs and lemon zest, which may be used in cooking recipes. Restrain for several times using successively finer strainers, or fine cloth. For maximum clarity, let liqueur stand for several days between strainings. Pour liqueur into bottles and cap.

* TIP: Pour some **Figgy Brandy** over your favorite fruit cake or figgy pudding for a special holiday dessert.

CHRISTMAS SPICED BRANDY

A holiday recipe from herbalist Terry Tucker Francis. A wonderful gift for the holidays, but you'll enjoy it so much, you'll want to serve it year-round. Ready in 1½ months. Makes about 1 fifth.

3 tablespoons mixed spices (any combination of broken cinnamon
    sticks, cracked allspice, cloves, allspice berries, grated ginger root
    or fresh nutmeg*)
colored peel only of ½ tangerine, minced
2 juniper berries
2 cups quality brandy or cognac
¾ cup brown cane sugar
½ cup granulated cane sugar
½ cup water

Combine chosen spices, tangerine peel and juniper berries with brandy or cognac in a 1-quart or larger aging container. Cap and store in a cool, dark place, shaking container and tasting once weekly for up to 3 weeks (until flavor is at its peak). Strain off spices and tangerine peel by pouring through muslin cloth or coffee filter paper. into a large bowl. Discard spices and peel. Clean out aging container. Re-strain until clear. Place strained liquid in clean aging container.

Combine sugars and water in a small saucepan. Heat over medium heat, stirring constantly to combine. When sugars are completely dissolved, remove from heat and let cool. Slowly add cooled sugar mixture to liqueur liquid, stir well. Age an additional 3 to 4 weeks to age and mellow.

* **TIP:** Use only 1 or 2 cloves or allspice berries and a single scraping of nutmeg. Too much of these potent spices could overwhelm subtler flavors.

GRAND ORANGE-COGNAC LIQUEUR

Our version of Grand Marnièr® is made with a good cognac or French brandy. Ready in 5 months. Makes about 1 pint.

⅓ cup orange zest*
½ cup granulated cane sugar
2 cups cognac or French brandy
1 tablespoon glycerin

Place zest and sugar in a small bowl. Mash together with the back of a wooden spoon or pestle. Continue until sugar is absorbed into the zest. Place in aging container. Add cognac. Stir, cap and age in a cool, dark place 2 to 3 months. Shake monthly.

After initial aging, pour through fine mesh strainer placed over medium bowl. Rinse out aging container. Pour glycerin into aging container and place cloth bag inside strainer. Pour liqueur back through cloth bag. Stir liqueur with a wooden spoon. Cap and age 3 more months before serving.

*NOTE: Seville oranges produce the authentic flavor but any type of orange peel/zest may be used with good results.

BRANDIED ESPRESSO LIQUEUR

A simple brandy liqueur that's a hit with coffee lovers, who sometimes have a difficult time waiting patiently for it to age! The coffee adds a depth and richness to the brandy that is very pleasant to the palate. Makes just over 1 quart.

> 2 tablespoons powdered espresso
> ½ cup boiling water
> 1 cup granulated cane sugar
> 1 vanilla bean, split lengthwise
> 3 cups brandy
> 1 to 2 teaspoons glycerin (optional)

In a small saucepan or microwave-safe bowl, dissolve the espresso powder in the boiling water. Stir in the sugar and vanilla bean and heat until mixture almost reaches a boil and the sugar is dissolved. Pour into an aging container and age for 1 to 2 months.

After preliminary aging, remove the vanilla bean, strain through several layers of cheesecloth and rebottle. Age an additional 2 months for best sipping, or 1 month if used for cooking.

*NOTE: Do not used ground espresso beans as they will not sufficiently infuse. Instant-dissolving powdered espresso can be found in the coffee section of the supermarket. It is possible to use instant coffee in this recipe, but the resulting liqueur will have significantly less coffee flavor.

BRANDYTOPF

Who among us is old enough to remember the wonderful days of Rumtopf, when it seemed as though everyone had a crock of it in the aging progress. Our version is updated for the 21st century, with a bright, new, sophisticated flavor you're sure to enjoy! For traditionalists, we've included a recipe for Rumtopf as well, although feel free to experiment with a combination of both alcohol bases.

Long ago a tradition was started by the Danes and Germans as a method to preserve the glorious flavors of summer fruits in alcohol and sugar. After several months of aging the products may be joyfully eaten as a dessert and liquid imbibed.

The Danes called it Romkrukke, while the Germans called it **Rumtopf**, both names literally mean rum pot in English. The name stuck, even though brandy or rum may be used to make it. There are stoneware Rumtopt containers available to make this in if you wish to be authentic, but it is not essential as other containers of glass or stoneware will do.

This classic fruit dessert and beverage is experiencing a resurgence in popularity due to its amazing taste, the fun of making it (especially if you grow your own fruits) and the feeling of satisfaction from making something uniquely yours to taste and share. It is wonderful in the winter months and has been traditionally served or gifted during the holidays, but is not limited to these times of year.

When your Fruited Brandy or Rum Mixture (Romkrukke or Rumtopf) is ready serve the Brandy or Rum soaked fruit over ice cream, pound cake, or special waffles perhaps topped with whipped cream as a very special dessert.

You may then drink the divine liquid which is your own unique fruit flavored liqueur or cordial. Makes wonderful gifts as well.

What you will need to make a Brandytopf or Rumtopf:

- 3 cups berries, plus later other mixed fruits in season, preferably organic
- A good quality Brandy or Rum,* enough to cover fruit
- Cane sugar, preferably organic, white or brown
- An aging container, glass or stoneware with a cover/lid or plate if there is no lid. A lid of some kind is essential to avoid evaporation.
- A cool, dark place to store it while aging

*NOTE: *Good quality brandy, 80-proof (40% alcohol/volume) or rum, at least an 80 proof, should be used. Avoid the 151-proof as it is highly flammable and is too strong. A mixture of the two may be used. If a stronger proof is desired, use a ratio of 1 part of 151-proof to 2 parts 80 proof.*

Fruits that may be used:

Apples, cored and sliced
Apricots, pitted and sliced
Blackberries, Blueberries, Gooseberries - pierced
Strawberries - hulled
Raspberries
Cherries, pitted
Currents, fresh Black or Red, pierced
Figs, sliced

Grapes, pierced if seedless, slice and remove seeds if any
Peaches, pitted and sliced
Pears, cored and sliced
Pineapple, outer peel and core removed, slice center
Plums, pitted, do not need to peel
Mangos, pitted and sliced
Nectarines, pitted and sliced
Walnuts, chopped, nuts are optional

Raisins, Currents and other dried fruits, whole unless large

Fruits best avoided:

Bananas, tend to overpower other flavors
Melons, all varieties

Directions for Fruited Brandy or Rum (Romkrukke or Rumtopf):

Ready your 2-gallon aging container/crock of glass or stoneware. (You may halve or quarter this recipe if your container is smaller.)

Begin with adding to a medium bowl:

3 cups berries, that have been washed & drained and
1½ cups sugar of choice, mixed gently with berries

Cover with plastic wrap and let stand several hours or overnight before adding other fruits.

Add berry mixture and juices to the aging container. Pour enough Brandy or Rum into container to cover fruit. Place a small plate on top of fruit to keep it submerged in the alcohol-sugar mixture to avoid any spoilage. Cover with lid and place in a cool, dark place.

The two ingredients, sugar and alcohol are your preservatives. In addition the sugar helps develop the flavor and keeps the alcohol from drawing all the flavor out of the fruits so they are enjoyable to eat later.

As other fruits are available add 2 cups of each chosen fruit, plus 1 cup sugar, adding directly to the aging container, stirring gently to combine. Again add Brandy or Rum to cover fruit added. Repeat process with other fruits 8 to 12 times, using the same measurements.

When your fruits are complete, or out of season, let mixture continue to age in its cool dark place for a month or two. It is then ready to serve. Enjoy!

SERVING &
MIXING LIQUEURS

SERVING & MIXING LIQUEURS

Most liqueurs are excellent mixed in cocktails or punches. We particularly like the fruit liqueurs in tropical drinks and punches. A good example of this type of beverage is in **Long Life Wedding Punch,** an elegant punch for any special occasion.

Traditionally, liqueurs are served at room temperature in small, stemmed liqueur glasses. Some liqueurs, such as **Amaretto,** can be served lightly warmed in a brandy snifter (small portions, please). Liqueurs are commonly served with after-dinner coffee but you will find many other special times and ways to serve them.

Some liqueurs, usually the herb-based recipes that are less sweet, are served with appetizers. An example would be the caraway-based liqueur, **Kümmel.** Some strong-flavored liqueurs, such as **Ouzo** or **Aquavit,** are also best served before a meal. Pair these liqueurs with appetizers of hot or cold cheeses, as well as seafood, for a perfect match.

AMERICAN WHISKEY PUNCH

An easy-to-make and refreshing punch. Makes just over 1 gallon.

1 fifth whiskey
3 ounces Curaçao or other Orange Liqueur
6 ounces California Lemon Liqueur
4 cups orange juice
1 quart iced tea
1 lemon, sliced
1 lime, sliced
1 quart club soda
ice

Combine first 5 ingredients in punch bowl. Decorate with fruit. Add soda and ice before serving.

A CONGRATULATORY TOAST

You have deserved high commendation,

true applause and love.

William Shakespeare, *As You Like It*, Act I

BANANA DAIQUIRI

*The addition of **Cherry Liqueur** gives this classic a new refreshing twist!
Serves 1.*

> juice of 1 lime
> 1 teaspoon granulated cane sugar
> 1-inch slice of banana
> 1 ounce light rum
> dash of **Cherry Liqueur**
> shaved ice
> 1 maraschino cherry with stem

Blend all ingredients, except cherry, in a blender or food processor. Pour into a chilled stemmed glass. Top drink with a stemmed cherry.

BITTER LEMON HIGHBALL

*Vary the flavor of this favorite drink by changing the variety of liqueur. We're especially partial to **Tropical Mango** or any citrus liqueur.*

Pour 1½ ounces of your favorite sweet liqueur into a highball glass. Add ice and fill with Bitter Lemon soda. Stir Well.

ISLAND PUNCH

A perfect adult punch for a summer party, yet ingredients are available any time of year to bring back the feeling of summer. Bring out your prettiest large punch bowl and fill with this liqueur laced fruity delight. Yield: about 20 servings.

    1 (64-ounce) can frozen pineapple juice, prepared
    1 pint (16 ounces) orange juice, fresh preferred
    ⅓ cup lemon juice, fresh preferred
    2 cups **Hawaiian Fruit** or **Pineapple Plantation Liqueur**
    ½ cup any **Orange Liqueur** or **Taboo Liqueur**
    ½ cup **California Lemon, Tony's Key Lime, Tropical Mango** or
       Piña Colada Liqueur
    1 orange, (a blood orange is striking), washed, halved, seeded and
       thinly sliced
    1 bottle (about 1 quart) of sparkling mineral water or lemon-lime
       soda

Chill all ingredients well before beginning. Prepare, chill and set aside orange. Set aside sparkling mineral water.

In a large punch bowl, combine pineapple juice, orange juice, lemon juice, and liqueurs. Stir gently. Cover and chill if not serving immediately.

When ready to serve: Pour in sparkling mineral water and stir gently. Float orange slices and ice block or ring on punch. Serve in punch cups or wine glasses.

NOTE:

Ice Block (optional): If you are going to use an ice block or ring, plain or decorated with fruit or flower petals, make this several days ahead.

CARIBBEAN COOLER

Straight from an island paradise, the perfect cooler for hot summer days. Serves 1.

1½ ounces rum (light or dark)
2 ounces (¼ cup) fresh or frozen strawberries, icy but thawed
1 ounce **Banana Liqueur**
1 ounce sweet and sour drink mix
crushed ice

Combine all ingredients in a blender or food processor. Blend until smooth. Pour into a tall chilled glass.

HARVEY WALLBANGER

*If you're fond of Harvey Wallbangers, whip up a batch of **Italiano Gold Liqueur** and try this easy recipe. Serves 1.*

1 ounce vodka
orange juice
½ ounce **Italiano Gold Liqueur**

Pour vodka into tall glass filled with ice cubes. Fill glass ¾ full with orange juice. Stir. Float or stir in **Italiano Gold Liqueur** as desired.

LIQUEUR FRAPPÉ

So easy, but very elegant. Serves 1.

Fill a stemmed glass with crushed ice. Pour 1½ ounces of your favorite liqueur over ice. Serve.

KIR

Kir, a French aperitif, is traditionally made with a dry white wine and **Crème de Cassis.** *We have found that a number of liqueurs, especially fruit liqueurs may be substituted for flavor variety. Try your favorites served in a champagne glass or flute with either a slice of fruit, fresh strawberry or a twist of lemon. Or add a bit of club soda to this for bubbles! Easy and lovely. Serves 2.*

6 ounces dry white wine of choice, chilled
1 ounce **Black Currant Liqueur** or fruit liqueur of choice

Combine, garnish and serve.

A TOAST OF FRIENDSHIP

May the hinges of friendship never rust,
nor the wings of love lose a feather.

Dean Ramsay

LIQUEURS ON ICE

A light cocktail or summer cooler may be made very simply with a variety of liqueurs. Fill an old-fashioned glass with ice cubes. Pour liqueur of your choice over and serve.

LONG ISLAND ICED "TEA"

This drink is served just like iced tea, in frosty pitchers and tall glasses with ice. Refreshing, but potent, this popular cocktail actually contains no tea at all! Serves 4.

⅓ cup **Orange Curaçao** or **Grand Orange-Cognac Liqueur**
¼ cup cranberry juice
¼ cup light rum
¼ cup tequila
½ cup vodka
ice cubes

Combine all ingredients in a pitcher. Add ice cubes to fill the pitcher; stir mixture well. Serve in highball glasses.

MAI TAI

Here's the Mai Tai you know and love, even better with your own liqueur! Serves 1.

1 ounce light rum
½ ounce **Orange Curaçao Liqueur**
¼ ounce orgeat syrup (available at liquor stores)
½ ounce orange juice
½ ounce lime juice

Combine all ingredients in a double old-fashioned glass with ice. Squeeze some lime juice into the drink and drop the lime shell into the glass. Garnish as desired with cherry, orange slice and pineapple.

PLUM SPARKLER

A summer refresher! Serves 1.

> 5 ounces white wine (such as a **Chablis**), chilled
> ice cubes
> 1 ounce **Plum Liqueur**
> 1½ ounces club soda
> 1 twist of lemon peel

Pour wine over ice cubes in a tall, chilled glass. Stir in Plum Liqueur and soda. Top with lemon twist and serve.

RAMOS FIZZ

A classic drink. Serves 1.

> 1½ ounces gin or vodka
> 1 ounce **any Orange Liqueur**
> 3 ounces half-and-half cream
> juice of half a lemon
> 1 egg white*
> 1 tablespoon powdered sugar
> ¼ cup shaved ice

Combine all ingredients in blender or food processor. Blend until smooth and frothy. Pour into tall chilled glass. Optional: Sprinkle a bit of ground nutmeg on top.

*NOTE:

For recipes including raw eggs, we advise using the whites of clean, uncracked pasteurized eggs, which can be found in some stores. Please read the note on page 59, concerning the possible danger of consuming raw eggs.

RHUBARB COOLER

This tall, cool drink is unexpectedly good! Serves 1.

Rhubarb Liqueur
orange juice
shaved ice
club soda

Combine equal amounts of Rhubarb Liqueur and orange juice. Pour enough of this mixture into a tall chilled glass filled with shaved ice until ⅔ full. Add enough club soda to fill glass.

SANGRIA

Mix this in a large pitcher in front of your guests for party flair. Makes about 2 quarts.

1½ cups cracked ice
½ cup **Orange Curaçao** or **any other Orange Liqueur**
½ cup **California Lemon Liqueur**
1 fifth red wine (Burgundy or red table wine preferred)
2 thinly sliced oranges
1 thinly sliced lemon
2 tablespoons granulated cane sugar
1 to 2 cups club soda

Place ice in pitcher. Combine all ingredients. Stir and serve.

STRAWBERRY MARGARITA

A favorite classic! Serves 1.

> 1½ ounces tequila
> ¾ ounce **Strawberry Liqueur**
> 6 to 8 fresh strawberries
> splash of sweet and sour mix
> shaved ice

Blend in a shaker, blender or food processor. Serve in a stemmed glass.

FORBIDDEN FRUITS COCKTAIL

An elegant, fruity drink, perfect for a special evening of entertaining. This easy make-ahead recipe is lovely served in champagne flutes. Serves 8-10.

> ⅓ cup orange juice, fresh is preferred
> 2 cups white Rhine wine, well chilled
> ¼ cup Cherry Liqueur
> ⅛ cup Black Currant Liqueur
> ⅛ cup lemon juice
> 1 cup pineapple cubes, fresh or packed in natural juice
> 1 cup strawberries, fresh preferred
> ½ apple, diced
> 1 orange, peeled, sectioned, and cut into quarters
> 1-2 bottles champagne, well chilled (added just before serving)

Combine all ingredients except champagne in a large container, stir. Cover and chill 12 to 24 hours. Before serving, lift out fruit pieces; spear fruits with toothpick for garnish.

To serve, fill champagne flutes almost half full with liqueur mixture. Fill the rest of the glass with chilled champagne. Stir gently. Garnish with fruit and serve immediately.

LONG LIFE WEDDING PUNCH

This outstanding punch was created by Cheryl Long for her wedding reception when she married a man named "Long." But it fits everyone, since tradition now dictates a toast to "Long Life" for the bride and groom. It is a very special blending of fruit liqueurs, champagne, fresh fruits, soda and a bit of Caribbean rum. A superb punch for special occasions. Of special note is the Make Ahead Directions for the fruit base.

Recipe makes about enough for 1 large punch bowl. Increase as needed. Enjoy! Yields about 2 gallons.

Fruit Base:

Combine in a large bowl (to hold about 1 gallon):

> 1½ quarts white grape juice
> 1 cup powdered sugar
> 1 cup lemon juice
> ¼ cup maraschino cherry juice
> ½ cup grenadine
> 2 cups pineapple juice
> juice of 4 fresh oranges
> pineapple chunks, cut from 1 fresh pineapple

Stir to combine all ingredients. Refrigerate until needed (use in 24 hours), or follow *Make Ahead Directions*.

Make Ahead Directions for Fruit Base:

Follow directions but do not refrigerate. Instead place fruit base in freezing containers (allow ample air space for expansion, at least 1 inch depending upon size of container). Freeze. Two days before needed, place in refrigerator to thaw.

Bubbly Completion:

Combine base with the following in a large punch bowl and serve:

1 quart club soda, well chilled
2 cups rum, light or dark
½ cup **any Orange Liqueur**
½ cup **Pomegranate** or any **Cherry Liqueur**
3 bottles champagne, well chilled
ice block or ring (optional, but nice frozen with fruit slices)

WEDDING TOASTS

Grow old with me!
  The best is yet to be,
The last of life,
  For which the first is made.
Robert Browning

May we all live to be present
  At their Golden Wedding.
May you grow old on one pillow.
Armenian Toast

HOT BUTTERED RUMTOPF or BRANDYTOPF

*When winter evening closes in, dark and chilly, nothing warms the soul more quickly than a small cup of **Hot Buttered Rumtopf or Brandytopf**, with a cocktail skewer of fruit from the **Rumtopf** or **Brandytopf** (page 91) for an appealing presentation. Recipe makes one 5-oz cup, but is easily doubled or tripled as desired.*

1 tablespoon butter, salted or unsalted
2 ounces liqueur from **Rumtopf** or **Brandytopf**
3 ounces boiling water
sprinkle of nutmeg
3 pieces of **Rumtopf** or **Brandytopf** fruit

In a small 5-oz cup or punch glass, place butter and the liqueur drained from your Rumtopf or Brandytopf crock. Add boiling water, stir until butter melts, then sprinkle a dash of nutmeg on top.

Thread fruit on a short cocktail stirrer or skewer, and place inside cup.

A CHRISTMAS TOAST

Here's to us all

God bless us every one!

Tiny Tim's Toast
From Charles Dickens' *A Christmas Carol*

CHRISTMAS CRANBERRY PUNCH

A bright and festive punch that brings sparkle to the season. Easily made from supplies that can be kept on hand. Recipe makes about 3 quarts, increase as needed.

> 1 quart cranberry juice, well chilled
> 1 quart lemon-lime soda, well chilled
> 1 cup vodka
> 2 tablespoons lime juice
> 1 cup **Cranberry Liqueur**
> ½ cup **any Orange Liqueur**
> 1 fresh orange, sliced
> granulated sugar, optional, to sweeten to taste if desired

Combine all ingredients, except orange slices, in a punch bowl. Add ice block or ring and fresh orange slices. Serve.

HOLIDAY TOAST

May you be poor in misfortune this Christmas and rich in blessings,
slow to make enemies, quick to make friends
and rich or poor, slow or quick,
as happy as the New Year is long.

Irish Toast

LIQUEUR COFFEE

*After-dinner liqueur coffee is easy to make when you have a selection of liqueurs on hand. Coffee served in this manner provides an elegant finish to a meal and may often be substituted for dessert. If your liqueur dictates, you may wish to top your coffee with sweetened whipped cream or **Whipped Liqueur Cream**. This may be served in demitasse or coffee cups, mugs, footed coffee cups or glasses, depending upon the occasion.*

*While almost any liqueur works well with coffee, some of our favorites are: **Amaretto, Crème de Menthe, Cherry, Irish Cream, Mexican Coffee, Old jamaican Coffee, Orange Curaçao** and **Scottish Highland Liqueurs**. Recipe makes about enough for 1 coffee cup or 2 demitasse cups. Makes about 6 ounces.*

> 5 ounces hot, freshly-brewed coffee
> ½ jigger (¾ ounce) liqueur of choice

Brew coffee to strength desired. Pour liqueur into coffee cup(s). Pour coffee over liqueur; stir to blend. Top with either sweetened whipped cream or Whipped Liqueur Cream (see page153) if desired. Serve immediately.

LIQUEURED HOT CHOCOLATE

*If you aren't a coffee lover, we suggest hot chocolate. The addition of a small shot of liqueur such as **Irish Cream, Mexican Coffee, Cherry**, etc, can turn an old standard into a hot drink with real pizzazz.*

SCANDINAVIAN SPICED COFFEE

A nice change of pace! Yield: 4 regular or 8 demitasse cup servings.

4 cups rich, hot coffee
1 cinnamon stick
6 whole allspice
⅛ teaspoon ground cardamom
¼ cup granulated cane sugar
4 fresh thin orange peel strips
4 tablespoons any **Orange Liqueur**
sweetened whipped cream, optional

Combine first six ingredients in medium saucepan. Heat gently, stirring to dissolve sugar. When heated through, turn off heat, cover and let stand for 15 to 20 minutes. Reheat and strain. Pour into 4 cups, put 1 tablespoon liqueur in each cup. Top with whipped cream, if desired, and serve immediately.

LIQUEUR MILKSHAKE

*This "adult" liqueur milkshake makes 1 serving. You may change the flavor of your milkshake by using any of the following liqueurs: **California Lemon, Crème de Menthe, Crème de Prunelle, Cherry, English Damson Plum, Hawaiian Fruit, Italiano Gold, Mexican Coffee, Old Jamaican Coffee, Orange Curaçao, Piña Colada, Taboo** or **Tropical Mango**.*

⅓ cup liqueur of choice
¼ cup crushed ice
1 scoop vanilla ice cream

Combine liqueur and ice in blender; process until well blended. Add ice cream and blend just until combined.

Serve immediately in a chilled goblet and garnish as desired with fresh fruit, chocolate curls, maraschino cherry, etc.

APERITIFS AND DIGESTIFS

Many liqueurs, primarily herbal ones, are often referred to as "aperitifs" or "digestifs." One of the best known is **Anisette,** with an anise or licorice flavor and a French name. Greek **Ouzo,** a stronger liqueur, also has an anise flavor. European caraway liqueurs are often called **Kümmel,** as is our German version. **Aquavit** is similar, but this Scandinavian aperitif is not sweet.

Aperitifs are generally served before a meal, often with appetizers or in place of them. The term "digestifs" refers to the digestive nature of some liqueurs. When used in this manner the liqueur is usually served after a meal. Either way, serve in small liqueur glasses, often chilled or on the rocks.

AQUAVIT IN AN ICE BLOCK

Aquavit should always be served ice cold. Here is a spectacular way to do so. Serve with appetizers, especially good with cheese and seafood.

Find a large, tall can that the Aquavit bottle will fit in comfortably. Pour about one-half inch of water in the bottom of the can and freeze the water (without the bottle in it this time). This forms a base. When water is frozen, place the bottle in the can and fill the can up with water. You may wish to add roses, ferns, herbs or other greenery or flowers for a decorative effect. Add about 1 inch of water to can, arrange plant material around bottle, then freeze all to hold in place. When frozen, fill can up with water and return to freezer with the bottle in it.

To serve, run hot water on the outside of the can for a few seconds until the ice melts just enough to release the ice block. Now wrap the base of the block in an attractive cloth napkin and pour for your delighted guests.

SKOALING

The popular Scandinavian toast is said in one word, *Skal,* or *Skol,* or as it has been anglicized, *Skoal.* Somewhat similar to our "cheers," but a bit rnore dignified, it generally means, "*A toast to you and your health.*"

COOKING
WITH
CLASSIC LIQUEURS

Cooking with Classic Liqueurs

COOKING WITH CLASSIC LIQUEURS

Making your own liqueurs is just half the fun. The other half lies in using your liqueurs to add a gourmet touch to your special dishes. Even everyday fare can undergo a transformation with the addition of a dash of liqueur. For example, baste your pork roast or pork chops with **Crème de Prunelle** before roasting or broiling and see what that little difference can do. When you are making gravy from the drippings, be sure to add a spoonful or two of **Crème de Prunelle** for flavor enhancement.

Baking opens up a whole realm of opportunities for using your homemade liqueurs. While most of the alcohol will evaporate if baked at higher temperatures, the essence of liqueur still adds flavor to the recipe. Many breads and muffins can be topped with a **Liqueur Glaze** (see page 149) which is not cooked and therefore keeps its full strength and flavor. Pie fillings offer the experimental cook a wide range of possibilities, One of our favorites is the addition of a couple of tablespoons of **Apple Liqueur** to apple, raisin or mince pie fillings. Extraordinarily good!

It's no accident that liqueurs are added to the recipes in this book. In developing them, we set high standards. Each recipe and liqueur is a marriage of flavors; one would not be complete without the other. This new edition of *Classic Liqueurs* includes eighteen exciting new food recipes as well as our favorites from the previous edition. We hope you'll have fun browsing through the recipes and starting with some that look appealing to you. In fact, we hope you'll try them all and discover how wonderfully versatile liqueurs can be.

SWISS DIAMONDS

These luscious onion and cheese appetizers flavored with caraway remind us of the Zurich region of Switzerland. Import them the next time you entertain. Can be made the day before so they are ready to bake. Serve hot with a chilled white wine. Makes about 3 dozen appetizers.

> 1 tablespoon olive oil
> 3 large onions, chopped
> 2 eggs, beaten
> 6 ounces Swiss or Gruyère cheese, shredded
> 8 ounces cream cheese, cut into chunks
> 2 tablespoons **Caraway Liqueur** or **Aquavìt**
> 1 teaspoon caraway seeds, bruised
> 9 sheets phyllo dough, about 14 by 18 inches
> 4 tablespoons butter, melted

Preheat oven to 375° F. Pour olive oil into a large frying pan, add onions and cook over moderate heat, stir often until lightly browned. Set aside.

Combine eggs, cheeses and liqueur and caraway seeds, stirring until well blended.

Lay out 3 sheets phyllo dough, brush melted butter lightly between each sheet. Place ⅓ of cheese mixture along one long edge of phyllo dough 1 inch in from edges. Brush 1-inch edge with extra butter down sides. Roll up jellyroll fashion, tucking the buttered edges in to hold in filling. Place on baking sheet and cover with plastic wrap to prevent dough from drying out. Repeat twice for a total of 3 rolls. Brush remaining butter lightly over tops of rolls.

Bake, uncovered, for about 15 to 18 minutes or until lightly browned. Let cool for 5 to 10 minutes, then slice each roll diagonally about 2 inches apart to make diamond-shaped appetizers. Serve hot.

continued

TIP:

If making appetizers ahead, cover unbaked rolls with plastic wrap and refrigerate until next day.

PLUM YUMMY SALSA

This yummy salsa fresca was developed especially for us by Lisa and Diane Gronholm, authors of the book, **Skinny Dips: Great Party Dips That Are (Secretly) Healthy**. *While the recipe calls for Plum Liqueur, it's also delicious made with other fruit liqueurs, such as* **Picante Pepper Liqueur**. *Serve it with tortilla chips or use as a relish with chicken or pork. Makes 2 cups.*

2 large red plums, finely chopped
1 large fresh apricot (or 4 dried apricot halves), finely chopped
1 firm medium tomato, finely chopped and drained
3 green onions, finely chopped
2 cloves garlic, finely chopped
⅓ cup green bell pepper, finely chopped
1 to 2 medium jalapeno peppers, finely chopped*
2 tablespoons **Plum Liqueur**
1 teaspoon rice vinegar
¼ teaspoon salt, or to taste
freshly grated black pepper, to taste

Combine all ingredients in a small mixing bowl. Cover and refrigerate at least two hours before serving, for flavors to reach their peak.

*NOTE: Jalapeno peppers vary greatly in their piquancy, depending upon their variety and growing conditions. When you buy them, you often have no idea how "hot" they are. If you like a mild salsa, use no more than one medium pepper. For a hotter salsa, more peppers can be added. But be careful! The salsa gets hotter as the flavors meld.

ROASTED PEPPER CHEDDAR SPREAD

This is a perfect make-ahead appetizer. Chill for at least four hours or overnight for the flavors to mingle. **Grand Orange-Cognac Liqueur,** *our version of Grand Marnier, adds that special flavor to this spread. Serve with crackers, toast, breads or vegetables. Makes about 1½ cups.*

⅓ cup (about two) roasted red peppers, peeled and chopped*
¼ cup mayonnaise (olive oil mayonnaise preferred)
1½ tablespoons **Grand Orange-Cognac Liqueur**
1 clove garlic, peeled and finely minced
1 teaspoon Dijon mustard
dash cayenne pepper
8 ounces grated sharp cheddar cheese

Mix all ingredients except cheese in a small mixing bowl. Add cheese and stir to combine; place in serving bowl. Cover and refrigerate at least 4 hours or overnight before serving.

*****NOTE:** Fresh or canned roasted peppers may be used in this recipe. If using canned peppers, drain juice first.

FRENCH COUNTRY PÂTÉ

An ideal recipe for entertaining. Easy when made in the food processor and best made ahead of time. The **Crème de Prunelle,** *a classic French prune liqueur, adds mellowness to this mildly flavored pâté. Serve with* **Seasoned Melba Toast.** *Makes about 2 cups.*

2 medium onions
cooking oil (canola, safflower or olive, preferred)
1 pound fresh chicken livers, washed and patted dry
flour
seasoning salt and pepper, to taste

1 tablespoon **Crème de Prunelle**

2 tablespoons cut liqueured prunes* (optional but good)

Peel onions and cut into fourths. Coarsely chop onions in a food processor with a steel knife. Place a thin layer of oil in a large frying pan. Add onions and sauté until medium brown in color. Remove onions from frying pan and set aside. Dip chicken livers into a mixture of flour, seasoning salt and pepper. Add additional oil to frying pan as necessary. Sauté chicken livers over medium-low heat until no pink remains.

Place cooked chicken livers, onions, Crème de Prunelle, prunes and any cooking oil left in pan (oil is optional) into the food processor work bowl. Process with steel knife until well blended, scraping down sides of bowl with spatula as necessary. Spoon into serving container. Pat flat on the top. Cover with plastic wrap and refrigerate 8 hours or overnight before serving.

*Prunes saved from making Crème de Prunelle.

SEASONED MELBA TOAST

The perfect accompaniment to **French Country Pâté**. *Simple, but delicious and economical to make.*

1 long French bread or baguette

seasoning salt or seasoning non-salt may be substituted

Preheat oven to 350° F. With a sharp knife, slice bread into ¼-inch thick slices. Lay slices on cookie sheets, spacing so sides do not touch. Lightly sprinkle all slices with seasoning salt. Bake for 20 minutes, or until lightly browned and dry to the touch. Remove from oven and let stand at room temperature until cool and crisp. Place in dry plastic bags. Seal and set aside until needed. May be made up to 1 week prior to use. Keeps well.

LIQUEUR GLAZED NUTS

*A special treat alone or use to top a gourmet sundae or cake. Experiment with your favorite liqueur flavors to see which you like the most. Two of our favorites to begin with are **Orange** and **Amaretto Liqueurs**. Fast and easy in the microwave oven. Makes about ½ cup.*

> ½ cup blanched nuts (almonds, filberts, etc.)
> 3 tablespoons **liqueur of choice**

Pour liqueur into a 9-inch glass pie plate. Add nuts and stir to coat very well. Microwave on HIGH (100%) power for 2 to 4 minutes, or until glazed and a light golden brown. Newer microwave ovens are higher power and may be ready in just 2 minutes. **Important:** Stop after each minute and stir.

The nuts will continue to toast after cooking. Spread on a plate or aluminum foil after nuts have cooled a minute or two. Cool further. Wrap up or store in an airtight container.

BREADS & SPREADS

ALMOND CREAM SCONES

Liqueur can be used as a flavorful extract as shown in this recipe. Use a more generous amount of liqueur when substituting for an extract as it is less concentrated. We like to leave scones in the round when serving, then cut into wedges while still warm. Serve with butter for breakfast or an afternoon tea. These are rich and flavorful enough that you may not need jam. Makes 8 scones.

> 2½ cups unbleached flour
> 2 teaspoons cream of tartar
> 1 teaspoon baking soda
> pinch of salt
> ⅓ cup sugar

4 tablespoons stick (½) butter or margarine
1 egg, beaten
¾ cup sour cream or half and half
3 tablespoons **Amaretto Liqueur**
½ cup sliced or slivered almonds, divided
1 tablespoon vanilla sugar or granulated sugar

Preheat oven to 350° F. Spray a baking sheet with vegetable coating spray or grease lightly.

Sift together flour, cream of tartar, baking soda and salt. Add sugar. Cut in butter with pastry blender or pulse in the food processor until a coarse-grained mixture forms. Stir in egg, sour cream and liqueur. Reserve 1 tablespoon almonds, gently stir in remaining almonds.

Turn scone mixture out onto a lightly floured board. Knead gently not more than 10 times.

We prefer to bake the dough in rounds, with wedges marked but not cut until after baking. Form the dough gently into a single round about ¾- to 1-inch thick and place on baking sheet. Sprinkle reserved almonds on top, pat into dough gently. Sprinkle sugar over top. With a floured knife cut through dough to pan to make 8 equal triangles but do not separate.

Bake in preheated oven until scones are a light golden brown, about 45 minutes. Let cool slightly for 5 to 10 minutes before serving. Cut into wedges while still warm.

HAZELNUT CREAM SCONES - Substitute chopped hazelnuts for almonds and **Hazelnut Liqueur** (our version of Frangelico) for the Amaretto Liqueur. Prepare as directed.

ORANGE FRENCH TOAST

For a special breakfast or brunch, serve this elegant variation of French Toast. May be served with butter and warm maple syrup, but we prefer it with **Whipped Liqueur Butter** *(page 125, try it with any* **Orange Liqueur***) and* **Warm Winter Berry Sauce** *(see page 138). Serves 4.*

6 eggs, beaten
1 teaspoon fresh orange zest*
½ cup fresh orange juice*
½ cup whole milk or half and half
⅓ cup any **Orange Liqueur**
1 teaspoon vanilla
8 slices thick bread (such as Egg, French or Cinnamon)
butter, as needed

Combine eggs, orange zest, juice, milk, liqueur and vanilla. When well combined dip bread into mixture. Either fry bread immediately on a preheated skillet with a small amount of butter or place dipped bread into a large baking dish in a single layer, cover and refrigerate until ready to cook in the morning. Serve hot.

*NOTE: One large fresh orange will supply the zest and juice for this recipe.

DID YOU KNOW...

That liqueurs make splendid extracts for cooking or baking. The heat during the cooking process will evaporate alcohol in foods containing liqueur, but will leave all the superb, aged quality of the ingredients. So cooked foods that have liqueur as an ingredient are perfectly safe for children.

LEMON LIQUEUR TEA LOAF

Use the aromatic liqueured lemon peels saved from making **Lemon Liqueur** *in this versatile tea-time favorite. Makes 1 loaf.*

½ cup (1 stick) butter or margarine
1 cup granulated cane sugar
2 eggs
½ cup milk
1 teaspoon baking powder
dash of salt, optional
1¼ cups sifted, all-purpose flour
½ cup finely chopped walnuts
5 tablespoons **Lemon Liqueur**, divided
2 tablespoons finely chopped lemon peel

Preheat oven to 350° F.

Soften butter. Cream sugar and butter together, then beat in eggs. Add milk to egg mixture.

Combine baking powder and salt with sifted flour. Stir flour mixture into egg mixture a little at a time, stirring well to combine. Finally, add nuts, 3 tablespoons Lemon Liqueur and lemon peel; stir well.

Spray a 5- x 9-inch loaf pan with vegetable coating spray or grease as desired. Bake for 55 to 60 minutes. Test with toothpick for doneness. Let cool. Poke a number of holes in the top of the loaf with a toothpick and pour 1 to 2 tablespoons Lemon Liqueur over the top. Serve warm or cool.

QUICK FRUIT LOAF

A favorite quick bread that can be made any time of the year. Use fresh cherries in season or substitute frozen or canned if out of season; delicious either way! We have even served it instead of the traditional fruitcake around the holidays. Even quicker when made in your food processor. Makes 1 loaf.

1½ cups all-purpose flour, sifted

1 tablespoon baking powder

½ cup granulated sugar (cane sugar preferred in this recipe)

½ cup (1 stick) butter or margarine

2 eggs, beaten or equivalent egg substitute

2 tablespoons **Cherry Liqueur** or other fruit liqueur

1 cup pitted cherries, fresh, frozen or canned*

⅓ cup raisins

⅔ cup mixed dried fruit

Preheat oven to 350° F.

Place flour, baking powder and sugar in a large mixing or food processor bowl. Mix dry ingredients. Cut butter into chunks and add to flour mixture. Cut in butter with pastry cutter or pulse with steel blade until mixture resembles coarse bread crumbs. If using food processor, remove mixture at this time and place in large bowl. Add eggs and liqueur; mix gently. Fold in all fruits.

Spray, with vegetable coating spray, or grease an 8" x 4" x 2" loaf pan. Pour mixture into pan. Bake for 55 to 60 minutes.

Test baked loaf with a wooden toothpick in the center. Will test clean when done. Remove from oven and let cool for 10 to 15 minutes before removing from pan. Serve plain or drizzle with **Liqueur Glaze** (page149), before serving.

*NOTE: If using canned cherries, drain well before adding to mixture.

WHIPPED LIQUEUR BUTTER

Another wonderful basic recipe you can have some fun with. Try a variety of flavors to find your favorites. Makes about ⅔ cup.

½ cup (1 stick) unsalted butter
1 tablespoon honey
¼ teaspoon grated fresh lemon peel
¼ cup **liqueur of choice**

Let butter reach room temperature. Combine all ingredients. Whip together until light and fluffy.

HEAVENLY CREAM CHEESE

We get so many raves over this very easy recipe, it's almost embarrassing! This can be used on almost anything. Excellent on nut breads. pound cake, cookies, crackers and simply wonderful used as a cake filling and/or frosting. Makes about 2 cups.

8 ounces cream cheese
½ cup confectioners' sugar
½ cup **liqueur of choice**
¾ cup chopped dried fruit*

Let cream cheese soften. Place in medium mixing bowl. Add sugar and half of the liqueur. Whip with whisk or beater. Add remaining liqueur, whip again. Check consistency, should be spreadable, add a small amount of liqueur if too thick. Fold in chopped fruit. Does thicken when refrigerated. Use as desired. Store in refrigerator.

*NOTE: A handy time-saver is to use the pre-chopped packaged dried fruit assortments now available in markets.

INTERNATIONAL CHEESE SOUP

*We paired Swiss cheese with Greek **Ouzo** and were rewarded with a hearty yet subtly flavored soup. A special bread and green salad served with this main dish soup make a memorable meal. Makes 10 cups.*

> 8 medium potatoes, peeled and diced
> 2 tablespoon butter or margarine
> 2 medium onions, chopped
> 3 cups chicken broth
> 2 cups grated Swiss cheese
> 3 cups milk
> 1 tablespoon **Ouzo Liqueur**
> chopped chives or croutons, as garnish

Place potatoes into a large soup pot. Cover with water and set aside While preparing onions. In a medium skillet, melt butter. Add onions and sauté until limp and transparent. Remove from heat.

Drain potatoes into a colander, discarding water, Return potatoes to pot and add chicken broth. Bring to a boil, lower heat and simmer, covered, until potatoes are soft. Remove from heat; stir in onions. Cool to lukewarm.

Using a blender or food processor, purée 2 cups of the potato mixture at a time until creamy and smooth. Repeat until all has been processed. Return to soup pot; add cheese and milk. Heat gently over medium-low heat, stirring often until cheese has melted and desired serving temperature is reached. (Do not allow soup to boil.)

Just before sewing, remove from heat and stir in Ouzo. Garnish with chopped chives or croutons as desired.

FRUIT SALAD ADVOCAAT

*An easy and creamy salad. Serve for breakfast, brunch, lunch or as a dessert. Great idea: substitute **Advocaat Liqueur** for cream or half and half in your favorite fruit salad dressing for a taste surprise. Serves 4.*

   1 quart prepared fresh mixed fruit, sliced or cubed
   ½ cup **Advocaat Liqueur**
   ½ to 1 cup whipped cream or topping (optional)

Combine all ingredients. Cover and chill 1 hour or more before serving.

LAYERED FRUIT SALAD WITH LIQUEUR

*A dazzling and unique make-ahead salad. Use a glass bowl and layer by colors for maximum effect. Vary the fruits used with the seasons as well as the fruit liqueur flavors. Some of our favorite liqueurs may get you started, such as: **Blackberry, Japanese Plum, Orange, Raspberry** and **Strawberry**. This can also be served as dessert, if desired. Serves 8 to 10.*

   2 bananas, sliced
   lemon juice
   confectioners' sugar
   1 pint strawberries, sliced
   2 oranges, sectioned
   1 to 2 cups pitted cherries
   2 apples or peaches or nectarines, sliced
   ¼ honeydew melon or pears or berries, sliced
   ½ cup **fruit liqueur of choice**

Place a layer of banana slices in a glass bowl. Lightly sprinkle with lemon juice, then cover with confectioners' sugar. Repeat in layers of fruit ending with sugar. Pour liqueur over all; cover and chill for 24 hours for best flavor.

FLAMING PINEAPPLE BOAT

This spectacular dish may be served as a fruit salad or dessert. Serves 4 to 8.

1 fresh pineapple, cut in half lengthwise
1 can (8 ounces) mandarin orange sections, drained
2 bananas, peeled and sliced
½ cup maraschino cherries, well-drained
⅓ cup **Orange** or **Highland Marmalade**
1 tablespoon **Pomegranate Liqueur**
¼ cup **Orange** or **Royal Anne Cherry Liqueur**
¼ cup sliced or slivered almonds
2 teaspoons butter or margarine
¾ cup shredded sweetened coconut
¼ cup rum

Cut gently all the way around each pineapple half leaving a ½-inch shell. Make two lengthwise cuts through the meat of the pineapple (one on each side of the core), leaving three long sections in each half. Gently remove the two side sections first, then the center section, leaving an attractive shell for serving. Slice each long section into cubes and place in a large bowl. Cut out core, discard. Drain pineapple cubes before proceeding.

Place drained pineapple in large mixing bowl and add orange sections, bananas, cherries, marmalade and fruit liqueurs. Stir to combine gently and set aside to let flavors blend.

Sauté almonds and butter in saucepan until lightly golden. Add almonds and coconut to fruit mixture; stir in gently. Divide mixture evenly between pineapple shells. Arrange for serving. Place on baking sheets and heat fruit boats in a 325° F oven for 25 minutes or until warm throughout. Place on serving dish.

Just before serving, heat rum slightly in saucepan or microwave. Pour rum over boats; light quickly. Allow flames to die out before serving.

TIP: May also be served cold. Don't heat or flame. Chill 2 hours.

ENTREES & SIDE DISHES

GERMAN APPLE PANCAKE PUFF

This recipe is a cook's dream. It's quick, easy to prepare, economical, absolutely delicious and a guaranteed "show-stopper." Try it as an entrée for a special brunch, breakfast or late supper. Serves 3 to 4.

 3 apples, peeled, cored and sliced
 3 tablespoons **Apple Liqueur**, spiced or unspiced
 6 eggs, separated
 ¼ cup all-purpose flour
 ¼ cup melted butter or margarine
 ¼ cup rich milk or half and half
 2 tablespoons butter or margarine

Topping:

 4 tablespoons sugar
 1 teaspoon ground cinnamon

Combine Topping ingredients. Set aside.

Preheat oven to 400° F. Place apples in medium mixing bowl. Pour liqueur over apples and stir gently to coat. Let stand while preparing pancake.

Beat egg yolks; mix in flour, melted butter and milk. Beat egg whites until they form stiff peaks. Fold beaten egg whites into flour mixture.

Heat 2 tablespoons butter in a large oven-proof skillet. When butter is melted, tilt pan to coat bottom and sides; pour in pancake batter. Spoon liqueured apples over top of batter to within ½-inch of edge.

Cook over medium heat for approximately 5 minutes. Transfer skillet to oven and bake for 15 minutes or until golden brown. Top with cinnamon-sugar topping mixture, cut into wedges and serve hot.

CRISPY GINGER ORANGE CHICKEN

A tangy orange-ginger sauce is a perfect companion to chicken. It's excellent served with risotto or rice pilaf and a leafy green salad. We like the zing of our **Grand Orange-Cognac Liqueur** *(a taste-alike to Grand Marnier) in this recipe but other orange liqueurs may be used in its place. Serves 4.*

2 sweet onions, such as Walla Walla or Vidalia

¼ cup olive or canola oil

4 half chicken breasts, boneless and skinless if preferred

½ cup milk

1½ cups cornstarch

½ cup flour

1 teaspoon salt

½ teaspoon freshly ground pepper

Sauce:

grated rind from 1 orange

1½ cups orange juice (juice from 3 large oranges plus water, if needed, to reach 1½ cups)

2 teaspoons cornstarch

⅓ cup **Grand Orange-Cognac Liqueur**

1 teaspoon grated fresh ginger

1 tablespoon granulated sugar

¾ teaspoon salt, or to taste

Preheat oven to 350° F. Cut onions into ½-inch slices. In a large non-stick skillet, sauté onions in the oil over medium heat for about 3 to 4 minutes, until they are partially cooked and slightly translucent. Transfer with a slotted spatula to a plate lined with a paper towel. Set aside. Save oil in pan for chicken.

Chicken breasts may be cut, if you wish, into smaller 2-inch pieces before cooking, or left in complete half-breast size. Pour milk into a small shallow bowl.

Combine cornstarch and flour in a separate bowl. Place half of this mixture in a one-gallon plastic bag. Dip half the chicken pieces into the milk, add to bag and shake. Repeat the process, coating the chicken twice. Then repeat with the remaining chicken and reserved flour.

Brown chicken pieces in the oil at medium heat, until lightly golden and crisp. Spread partially cooked onions in a large, flat baking dish. Arrange chicken pieces on top and bake, uncovered for 20 minutes (or 15 minutes if cut into small pieces). Wipe the skillet with a paper towel.

Meanwhile, prepare the sauce. Grate the peel of one orange and place in the skillet. Add the juice from the 3 oranges, reserving 2 tablespoons. In a cup, dissolve the cornstarch in 2 tablespoons of orange juice, then add this to the juice in the skillet, stirring well. Add remaining ingredients. Stir over medium-low heat until sauce begins to thicken.

When chicken has cooked for the required time, remove from oven and check the inside. If still pink, return to oven for another 5 minutes. When cooked, spoon sauce over chicken, but do not cover each piece entirely, so that it remains crisp. Return to oven for an additional 5 minutes.

PLUM GLAZED CORNISH HENS

Our cooking school favorite is wonderful for entertaining. Make with Cornish game hens, pheasant, whole or cut-up chicken. Serve with wild rice or a rice pilaf. Serves 4 to 8.

4 Cornish game hens or 2 roaster/fryer chickens
salt
dash white pepper
4 to 8 tiny onions, peeled
1½ cups pitted canned plums
¼ cup reserved plum juice
1½ tablespoons cornstarch
2 tablespoons lemon juice
3 tablespoons cane sugar
1½ tablespoons onion powder
¼ cup raisins
½ cup **Plum Liqueur**

Preheat oven to 350° F. Prepare poultry. Remove giblets from center cavity. Wash, pat dry. Lightly salt and pepper cavity. Place 1 to 2 onions inside each cavity. Tie legs together with string. Arrange in baking dish and set aside while making sauce.

Purée pitted plums in processor or blender. Combine reserved plum juice and cornstarch in a small bowl, mix well. Put lemon juice, sugar and onion powder in a small saucepan. Heat to a beginning boil and simmer until slightly thickened, stirring constantly. Remove from heat and stir in raisins and liqueur. Pour sauce over game hens. Cover and bake at 350° F about 1½ hours. Baste halfway through cooking and again near end.

*TIP: If using poultry parts, decrease time to about 1 hour. Check doneness.

continued

CLAY POT DIRECTIONS: An alternate method of cooking. Soak empty clay pot and cover in lukewarm water for 15 minutes. Drain off excess water by placing on clean toweling for a few minutes. Place poultry in pot. Pour sauce over and cover. Place clay pot in a cold unheated oven. Turn oven to 425° F. Bake 1 to 1¼ hours. Baste near end of cooking time.

MANGO CHUTNEY CHICKEN

A superb and colorful dish that is company-perfect, looks like you slaved all day, but cooks easily in one skillet. Add a green salad or vegetable and you have it! Serves 4.

> salt and pepper to taste
> 4 boneless, skinless chicken breasts
> 2½ cups yams or sweet potatoes
> 2 tablespoons canola or olive oil
> 1 large onion, thickly sliced
> 1 mango
> 1 cup orange juice
> ½ cup mango or other fruit chutney
> ¼ cup **any citrus liqueur**

Salt and pepper chicken breasts. Peel and cut yams into large chunks.

In a large skillet, add oil, chicken breasts and yams. Cook over medium heat, turning to brown sides.

Lay onion slices over chicken. Peel and cut mango into chunks and scatter over all. Pour orange juice over. Reduce heat to medium and cook for 10 minutes.

Spoon chutney onto chicken and onions. Pour liqueur over all. Cover skillet and simmer on low heat until chicken is thoroughly cooked and yams are tender.

ROAST PORK WITH DANISH CHERRY SAUCE

Pork roast is a classic Danish dish, often served at a special dinner. The spicy Cherry Sauce is the crowning touch to this dish. Conventional oven and microwave cooking directions are given. Serve with tiny oven browned potatoes. Serves 6 to 8.

Roast:
4 to 5 pounds center cut pork loin roast (boneless or bone-in)
teaspoon pepper

Preheat oven to 350° F. Lightly pepper pork loin on all sides. Place roast, fat side up, on roasting rack in open shallow roasting pan. Allow 30 to 35 minutes per pound and roast at 350° F until roast reaches an internal temperature of 165° F. (Test with a meat thermometer in the meaty center of the roast.) Remove from oven and let stand 15 to 20 minutes before serving. (Prepare sauce.)

Sauce:
½ cup red cherry preserves
¼ cup agave syrup, white corn syrup or light honey
1 tablespoon white or white wine vinegar
¼ cup **Cherry Liqueur**
⅛ teaspoon ground cinnamon
⅛ teaspoon ground cloves

Combine all sauce ingredients, except 2 tablespoons Cherry Liqueur, in a saucepan. Bring to a gentle boil and simmer for 1 minute. Remove from heat and stir in remaining liqueur. Spoon all or part over roast before serving. Serve with extra sauce, if any, on the side.

Microwave Directions:
Roast:
Lightly pepper pork loin on all sides. Place fat side down on a microwave roasting rack in a 2-quart or larger glass baking dish. Microwave on HIGH (100%) power for 20 minutes.

Next, turn roast fat side up. Microwave on MEDIUM-HIGH (70%) power for about 15 to 20 minutes or until center of meat reaches 160° F. (Be sure to use only a microwave meat thermometer or probe if checking temperature inside an operating microwave oven.) Remove from oven and place a loose cover tent of aluminum foil over roast and let stand for 15 to 20 minutes before serving.

Combine all sauce ingredients except 2 tablespoons Cherry Liqueur in a 4-cup glass measure. Microwave on HIGH power for 3 minutes. Stir in remaining liqueur. Serve as previously directed.

MANDARIN YAM BAKE

Tired of the traditional marshmallow/sweet potato dishes? We are! This recipe is guaranteed not to have a marshmallow in it, and is quite different and delicious. Serves 8.

5 cups (40-ounce can) cooked yarns or sweet potatoes, peeled, drained and mashed
¼ cup melted butter or margarine
⅓ cup **Taboo Liqueur** or **any Orange Liqueur**
1 small can (11-ounce) mandarin oranges, drained
⅓ cup firmly packed brown sugar
¼ cup chopped macadamia nuts, pecans or walnuts
1 tablespoon butter

Preheat oven to 375° F. Combine mashed yarns, ¼ cup melted butter and Taboo Liqueur in a 2-quart casserole dish; mix well. Gently fold in drained mandarin orange sections. Pat down evenly in casserole. Sprinkle brown sugar and nuts over top of casserole and dot with the one tablespoon of butter. Bake for 30 minutes.

Microwave Directions: Prepare as directed. Instead of baking, place into microwave-safe casserole dish; cover with waxed paper. Cook on HIGH (100%) power for 7 to 8 minutes. Quarter turn dish halfway through cooking time, as necessary. Let rest, covered, 5 minutes before serving.

LEMON-SCENTED CRÊPES

This is a wonderful dessert crêpe that can enhance many different fillings and toppings. Crêpes can be made several days ahead, wrapped well to prevent drying, refrigerated or frozen for several weeks. A delicious way to serve these crepes is with **Orange Cream Filling.** *You'll find the filling recipe and assembly instructions immediately following this recipe. Makes about 20 six-inch crêpes.*

4 eggs or 1 cup egg substitute
1 cup milk
3 tablespoons melted butter
3 tablespoons **Lemon** or any **Orange Liqueur**
1 cup all-purpose flour
2 tablespoons cane sugar
1 teaspoon grated lemon rind
dash of salt

Put all ingredients into a blender jar, cover and blend for 1 minute. Scrape down sides and blend for 1 minute more. Place covered blender jar in refrigerator, chill for at least 2 hours before making crêpes.

To cook crêpes, heat a 6- to 7-inch skillet or crêpe pan over medium heat. Spray with vegetable cooking oil and pour less than ¼ cup crêpe batter into pan. Tilt pan so that batter covers entire bottom of pan. Cook about 1 minute or until lightly brown then turn over and cook about 30 seconds. Remove crêpe to a plate and cover with waxed paper. Lightly re-spray pan as needed and repeat process.

ORANGE CREAM FILLING

*A perfect filling for **Lemon Scented Crêpes** but so good you will find other uses for this recipe as well. An excellent make-ahead recipe when company is coming. Makes about 2 cups*

8 ounces cream cheese, softened
1 cup sour cream
½ cup confectioners' sugar
1 tablespoon any **Orange** or **Lemon Liqueur**
grated rind of 1 small orange

Place cream cheese, sour cream, sugar and liqueur into a medium-sized mixing bowl. Whisk or beat until well blended and smooth. Stir in orange rind. Cover bowl and chill for at least 1 hour for flavors to blend. May be chilled overnight if desired.

LEMON-SCENTED CRÊPES WITH ORANGE CREAM FILLING

Prepare recipes above and combine as follows. Top with fresh berries, Lemon Sauce, Lemon Curd, Sweetened Whipped Cream or **Warm Winter Berry Sauce** (following page). Serves 10 people 2 crêpes each

To fill crêpes, place 2 rounded tablespoons of Orange Cream Filling down the center of each crêpe, fold half over filling then roll up crêpe. Place filled crêpe seam side down into a 9 x 13-inch baking dish. When assembled, cover pan to prevent crêpes from drying out.

To serve, preheat oven to 350° F. Place baking dish into oven and heat filled crêpes for10 minutes. Top crêpes as desired.

WARM WINTER BERRY SAUCE

This recipe may be made with frozen strawberries, raspberries, blackberries or blueberries. Gourmet sauce that can be made from frozen berries. Top crêpes, pound or other cakes, or ice cream for a special dessert. Makes about 3 cups sauce.

   1 orange
   2 tablespoons butter
   2 tablespoons lemon juice
   1 cup berries, puréed
   ⅔ cup granulated cane sugar
   3 cups berries, slightly mashed
   4 tablespoons **Raspberry, Strawberry** or any **Orange Liqueur** of
      choice

Grate rind of orange to obtain 2 tablespoons, set aside. Cut orange in half and juice orange. Remove any seeds. Set juice aside.

In a 2- or 3-quart saucepan, melt butter and stir in orange juice, lemon juice, puréed berries and sugar. Bring just up to a boil, stirring constantly until sugar is completely dissolved. Add 3 cups mashed berries and liqueur. Heat until small bubbles appear around edge of pan. Remove from heat and ladle hot sauce over heated filled crêpes, cake or ice cream.

TIP: If serving over ice cream, make sure ice cream is well frozen and sauce warm, not hot, when poured over. Serve immediately.

STRAWBERRY-DIPPING CREAM

*When strawberry season is at its peak, serve this delightfully different lemony dip with a bowl of whole fresh berries! Or use with angel food cake to make a **Lusciously Light Strawberry Shortcake**. Makes 2 cups.*

    1 cup low-fat, no-fat or part-skim ricotta cheese
    1 6-ounce container (¾ cup) of light lemon yogurt
    ¼ cup **Lemon Liqueur**
    2 teaspoons cane sugar
    2 teaspoons fresh or 1 teaspoon dried grated lemon peel

In a blender, combine ricotta, yogurt, liqueur and sugar. Blend until smooth. Transfer to a serving bowl and stir in lemon peel. Cover and refrigerate for an hour or two before serving to allow the flavors to mingle.

LUSCIOUSLY LIGHT STRAWBERRY SHORTCAKE

Not only is it very low in fat, but the best part is, you'd never know it! Makes 4 to 5 servings.

    2 pints (16 ounces) fresh strawberries, cleaned and sliced (save 5
        whole berries for garnish)
    2 tablespoons **Lemon Liqueur**
    1 teaspoon cane sugar
    1 angel food bar cake
    1 recipe **Strawberry Dipping Cream**

Place sliced strawberries in a small mixing bowl. Splash strawberries with liqueur, sprinkle sugar over and mix lightly. Refrigerate for an hour or two for best flavor.

To serve, place a slice of angel food cake on plate, top with strawberries and spoon chilled Strawberry Dipping Cream over top. Garnish each serving with a whole strawberry.

RICH CHOCOLATE LIQUEUR CAKE

I love this quick, made-from-scratch cake. The ingredients are on hand in my pantry so there are no special ingredients to purchase. It is elegant enough for company and is easy enough to make up on short notice. Divine served slightly warm. Top it with whipped cream for simple elegance or a simple scoop of vanilla ice cream. You may wish to drizzle a bit of the liqueur used over the whipped cream or ice cream as a luscious accent. Additional garnishes are: a fresh mint sprig or a bit of shaved chocolate on the whipped cream. Yield one 8" cake. Serves 6 to 8.

> 2 cups sifted cake flour
> 4 tablespoons cocoa
> 2 teaspoons baking powder
> ¼ teaspoon salt
> ⅓ cup unsalted butter, softened
> ¾ cup cane sugar
> 2 large or extra large egg yolks
> 1 cup milk, regular or 2%
> ¼ to ⅓ cup of your favorite flavor liqueur such as **Orange, Raspberry,**
>   or **Mexican Coffee**

Preheat oven to 325° F. Spray 8" cake pan with vegetable coating.

Sift and measure flour. Sift flour, cocoa, baking powder and salt together; set aside.

In medium bowl, cream butter and sugar together. Add egg yolks, mix to incorporate. Add half of the milk, beat well. Alternate in small amounts flour mixture and the remaining milk and liqueur; beat well after each addition. Pour into prepared pan. Bake for 45 minutes or until cake tests done.

APPLE PIE SNACK CAKE

The heady aroma of this fall and winter favorite has filled the air at so many of our cooking classes. This moist, easy-to-make "anytime" cake is especially welcome when the air is crisp. Bake it fresh or make ahead, freeze and reheat slightly to serve. Excellent for gift giving. Makes two 9-inch cakes.

Dry Ingredients:
- 1¾ cups granulated cane sugar
- 2 cups cake flour
- ½ cup golden seedless raisins
- 1 teaspoon ground cinnamon
- ¼ teaspoon ground cloves
- ½ teaspoon ground allspice
- 1½ teaspoons baking soda
- ½ teaspoon baking powder
- ½ teaspoon salt (optional)
- ⅛ teaspoon instant coffee
- Vanilla Sugar (see page 163) or confectioners' sugar

Liquid Ingredients:
- 2 eggs
- ½ cup spiced or unspiced **Apple Liqueur**
- ⅔ cup vegetable oil (for a lower fat version, substitute unsweetened applesauce for half or all of the oil)
- 2 cups apple pie filling

Preheat oven to 350° F. Grease and flour, or spray with vegetable coating, two round or square 9-inch cake pans. Combine all dry ingredients except Vanilla Sugar in a large mixing bowl; mix well.

In a medium mixing bowl, beat eggs. Add rest of liquid ingredients; stir well until combined. Pour liquid ingredients into dry ingredients. Beat well to completely mix, scraping sides occasionally. Pour into prepared pans. Bake for 50 to 55 minutes. Test with toothpick for doneness. Cool in pans on cake racks. When cooled, sprinkle with Vanilla Sugar.

AMARETTO-ALMOND TEA CAKE

This perfectly elegant cake contains the wonderful ingredients that made **Amaretto Liqueur** *famous: almonds and apricots. The liqueur itself adds a flavorful note to the cake and a richness to the special glaze. Just for fun, hide a whole almond in the batter before baking. The fortunate finder will have the best of luck for the next year! Makes one 8- to 9-inch cake.*

Cake:
- 1 cup butter or margarine
- 1⅓ cups granulated cane sugar
- 4 eggs
- ½ teaspoon almond extract
- 1 cup lemon yogurt
- 2 ½ cups all-purpose flour
- 1 teaspoon baking powder
- 1 teaspoon baking soda
- 1 cup finely chopped, blanched almonds
- 1 whole shelled almond (optional)

Drizzle:
- 1 tablespoon **Amaretto Liqueur**

Glaze & Decoration:
- ⅔ cup apricot jam
- 2 tablespoons **Amaretto Liqueur**
- ¾ cup finely chopped or slivered, blanched almonds
- ¾ cup whole blanched almonds (optional)

Preheat oven to 350° F. Generously grease an 8- to 9-inch springform pan. Cut a circle of waxed paper to fit the bottom of the pan; place it in the pan and grease the paper. Flour the pan.

Cream butter or margarine. Add the sugar and cream well. Beat in 1 egg at a time, until combined. Stir in the almond extract and yogurt. Add the dry ingredients, beating well. Mix in the 1 cup chopped almonds.

Pour into prepared pan, press the whole almond into the batter (if desired) and bake for 50 to 60 minutes, until cake tester comes out clean.

Cool in pan for 10 minutes; remove sides of pan and cool to lukewarm. Pierce top of cake with a fork at intervals, to a depth of ¼-inch. Drizzle liqueur over the surface of the cooled cake.

Force apricot jam through a wire-mesh strainer to obtain a smooth textured glaze or process in a food processor or blender. Add the 2 tablespoons Amaretto, mixing well to combine. Spoon ¾ of the glaze over the top and sides of the cake, covering the surface completely. Press chopped almonds to the sides of the cake and decorate the top with whole almonds in a starburst pattern or a design of your choice. Spoon the remaining glaze over the top decoration.

VARIATION: AMARETTO-ALMOND LAYER CAKE - Increase the apricot jam to 1 cup and combine this with 2 tablespoons plus 2 teaspoons **Amaretto Liqueur,** for the glaze. With a long knife, carefully split the cooled, undecorated cake into 2 layers. Drizzle each layer with 2 teaspoons Amaretto. Spread a layer of the glaze over one layer of cake and top with the second cake layer. Glaze and decorate according to directions above.

CITRUS LIQUEUR CAKE

*A flavorful, dense, old-fashioned type of cake that is wonderful made with any citrus flavors. Match the grated rind with the dominant flavor in the liqueur of choice, such as **Orange Liqueur** and grated orange rind. Serve plain or topped with **Citrus Liqueur Drizzle** or whipped cream. Makes one 8-inch tube or bundt cake.*

Cake:
¾ cup raisins
2 tablespoons **Taboo** or any **citrus liqueur**
1 cup (2 sticks) butter or margarine, softened
1½ cups granulated cane sugar
4 eggs
2 teaspoons baking soda
3½ cups cake flour
1⅓ cups buttermilk
¾ cup chopped walnuts
1 tablespoon fresh grated citrus rind, flavor of choice

Citrus Liqueur Drizzle:
½ cup orange or citrus juice
¼ cup **Taboo** or other **citrus liqueur** of choice

Preheat oven to 350° F. Grease or spray with vegetable coating an 8-inch tube or bundt pan. Set aside.

Plump raisins by pouring boiling water over, covering completely. Let sit 10 minutes. Drain off water. Pour liqueur over raisins and set aside until needed.

In a large mixing bowl, cream butter with sugar. Add one egg at a time until well mixed, scraping sides of the bowl with a spatula as needed. Add baking soda to butter mixture, stirring well. Alternate additions of flour and buttermilk to the mixture. Stir in walnuts, liqueured raisins and grated orange or citrus rind.

Pour mixture into prepared pan. Bake about 50 minutes or until cake tests done with a toothpick. Remove from oven, let cool a bit then poke cake with toothpick at ½" intervals.

In a small bowl, combine **Citrus Liqueur Drizzle** ingredients and drizzle over the cake.

CRÈME DE MENTHE FROSTING

A luscious and easy-to-make frosting that makes brownies or chocolate cake very, very special. Authors Joyce Webster and Susan Van der Velde shared this versatile recipe from their cookbook, **Try It, Like It! Microwave Desserts.** *The glaze can also be made in a double boiler. Enough to frost a 9-inch cake.*

Frosting:
⅓ cup butter
1½ cups confectioners' sugar
1 tablespoon corn syrup
2 tablespoons **Crème de Menthe Liqueur***
½ teaspoon vanilla extract
Chocolate Glaze:
½ cup chocolate chips
1 tablespoon butter
1 tablespoon milk

In a 4-cup measure combine butter, sugar, corn syrup, Crème de Menthe and vanilla. Stir until smooth and creamy. In a separate measure combine chocolate chips and butter. Microwave uncovered, on HIGH (100%) power for 1 minute or until chocolate has melted. (Stir to test melting.) Stir in milk until smooth. Spread Crème de Menthe frosting over top of brownies or cake. Drizzle Chocolate Glaze in a criss-cross fashion over frosting. Refrigerate.

***TIP: Fresh Mint Liqueur** may be substituted for the **Crème De Menthe Liqueur.**

CHOCOLATE NUT RUFFLE

Any cookbook worth its salt has at least one very special recipe. This is it! We have had more compliments on this dessert than we can count. A caterer selected this recipe and served it to a conference of over 250 librarians. (Our library book sales went up dramatically!) We can only say, if you like chocolate, do try it. Rich and wonderful, it is pretty served in demitasse cups or small, footed glasses. Makes 8 demitasse servings.

1 cup superfine or regular granulated cane sugar
¾ cup cocoa powder (fine Dutch cocoa preferred)
½ cup **Old Jamaican Coffee Liqueur**
4 egg yolks
1 cup whipping cream
½ cup chopped almonds, toasted
¾ cup coarsely chopped semi-sweet chocolate
semi-sweet chocolate shavings for garnish

In the top portion of a double boiler, combine the sugar, cocoa and liqueur. Cook over medium heat 15 minutes, stirring constantly.

In a large bowl, beat the egg yolks until slightly fluffy, about 1 to 2 minutes. Slowly drizzle the hot chocolate mixture into the beaten yolks, beating to combine. Beat for 2 minutes more, scraping sides of bowl as needed. Refrigerate until cold (30 to 45 minutes).

Whip cream until stiff peaks form. Add a spoonful of whipped cream to the chocolate mixture and stir in to soften the chocolate. Fold in the remainder of the whipped cream, very gently. Add almonds and chopped chocolate, stirring just enough to combine. Be careful not to disturb the fluffiness of the whipped cream.

The mixture may be frozen at this point. Cover bowl or fill cups or glasses with mixture, allowing about cup per serving. Garnish with chocolate shavings and cover and freeze. Freeze at least 2 hours before serving. Serve frozen.

ITALIAN ANISE STARS

These tiny, buttery, melt-in-your-mouth stars have just the merest tantalizing hint of Anisette. Makes 9 dozen tiny stars.

1 cup butter
⅓ cup golden brown cane sugar
2¼ cups all-purpose flour
2 tablespoons **Anisette Liqueur**

Preheat oven to 325° F. In a mixing bowl, cream the butter; add the sugar gradually, combining thoroughly. Mix in half of the flour until dough is smooth, then add the liqueur, beating until well blended.

Sprinkle the remaining flour over a pastry cloth or smooth rolling surface until the excess flour has been worked into the dough. Refrigerate dough at least 1 hour for easier handling.

On a lightly floured surface, roll dough to ¼-inch thickness. Use a 1¾-inch cookie cutter dipped in flour to cut the tiny star-shaped cookies. Transfer to an ungreased baking sheet; bake for 12 minutes or until just the edges are a light golden brown.

VARIATION: For a moist cookie with a more pronounced anise flavor, brush the tops of the stars while still hot, with a glaze made from one teaspoon granulated cane sugar combined with 2 teaspoons Anisette Liqueur.

BRANDIED FRUITCAKE COOKIES

*A special holiday cookie. Plan ahead on these cookies as the candied fruits need to soak in the **Fruit Brandy** for 24 hours before preparation. Select your favorite candied fruit(s) for these cookies or use a mixed candied fruit mixture. Yield: 4 dozen cookies.*

2⅓ cups mixed candied fruit
1 cup raisins, any kind
⅓ cup **Pear Brandy,** or any other fruit Brandy you prefer

Day One:
Add candied and dried fruit to a medium size bowl. Pour pear brandy over fruit and gently stir to combine. Cover bowl with waxed paper or plate to fit. Stir the brandy fruit mixture several times over the 24 hours.

Day Two:
2 large eggs
½ cup packed dark brown cane sugar
5 tablespoons butter or vegan alternative, melted
½ teaspoon baking soda
1 teaspoon ground cinnamon
½ teaspoon ground cloves
½ teaspoon ground nutmeg
1 teaspoon vanilla extract
1½ cups unbleached all-purpose flour or white spelt flour, sifted
1 cup chopped pecans or walnuts

Preheat oven to 375° F.

In a large bowl, beat eggs with sugar until combined. Add melted butter, baking soda, cinnamon, cloves, nutmeg and vanilla, mixing well. Add in the flour in four equal amounts, mixing well after each amount.

Add brandied fruits, brandy liquid and nuts. Gently combine until all is well mixed.

Spoon rounded teaspoonfuls onto one or two ungreased baking sheets. Bake cookies about 15 minutes, or until they are lightly browned. Remove from oven and cool.

THE MAGIC OF LIQUEURS

Liqueurs offer a delightfully expanded palette of flavors in cooking and baking. For example, if your recipe calls for lemon extract, try **California Lemon Liqueur** *instead. Or substitute* **Mexican Coffee Liqueur** *or* **Old Jamaica Coffee Liqueur** *for recipes that call for a coffee flavor.*

It's fun to combine two different liqueurs in cooking to create entirely new and rich flavor combinations. **Apple Liqueur** *and* **Amaretto** *are two than work beautifully together, and* **Picante Pepper Liqueur** *lends a spicy undertone when used in cooking paired with* **Orange Liqueur.**

LIQUEUR GLAZE

So useful for a quick glaze, drizzle or use as a special topping on many baked items. Makes about ¼ cup.

½ cup confectioners' cane sugar
3½ teaspoons **liqueur of choice**

Place ingredients in a small bowl. Combine and beat with a whisk or beater until smooth.

ENGLISH APRICOT TRIFLE

If you enjoy a traditional English Trifle, you will find our version laced with liqueur irresistible. Serves 10.

Base:
  1 standard size loaf pound cake*
  4 teaspoons sherry
  ½ cup **Plum** or **Apricot Liqueur,** divided
  1 (12-ounce) jar apricot preserves

Custard:
  1 envelope (3 tablespoons) Birds English Custard
  3 tablespoons cane sugar
  2 cups milk

Garnish:
  1 teaspoon butter
  2 tablespoons slivered almonds
  1 red maraschino cherry, optional

Whipped Cream Topping:
  ½ pint whipping cream
  2 tablespoons cane sugar
  ¼ teaspoon vanilla

Cut pound or sponge cake into 3/4" x 2" slices or strips. Cut again to make each piece about 2 inches long. Place half of cake pieces into bottom of trifle or 2-quart glass bowl. Sprinkle 2 teaspoons sherry and ¼ cup liqueur over cake. Spoon half the apricot jam over all.

Prepare custard as package directs, using milk and 3 tablespoons sugar. Pour half of the hot custard over base layer.

Repeat directions to create a second cake layer. Pour remaining hot custard over second layer. Cover bowl with plastic wrap and refrigerate.

For Garnish: Place almonds and butter in small saucepan. Cook over medium heat, stirring constantly until almonds are lightly toasted. Remove from heat and let cool.

For Whipped Cream Topping: Whip cream until soft peaks form. Mix in vanilla and 2 tablespoons sugar. Spoon sweetened whipped cream over top of trifle. Sprinkle cooled almonds over. Top with cherry. Re-cover and chill for 2 hours before serving.

*TIP: A 9 ½ x 14-inch sponge cake may be substituted for the pound cake if preferred.

CHOCOLATE ORANGE FONDUE

Fantastically quick and sinfully good! A "must-do" recipe! Dip assorted fresh fruits into this fondue or use as a warm sauce over ice cream or frozen yogurt. Refrigerates and reheats well. Makes over 1 cup.

    ½ cup whipping cream
    2 tablespoons any **Orange Liqueur**
    2 bars (4 ounces each) German chocolate, broken into pieces

Combine all ingredients and cook in a double boiler, stirring constantly, until smooth and satiny. Serve warm.

Microwave Directions: In a 1-quart or larger glass bowl combine cream and liqueur. Add chocolate pieces. Microwave on MEDIUM-HIGH (70%) for 2½ to 3 minutes, stirring halfway through cooking time. Remove from microwave oven. Stir or whisk until smooth. If some chunks remain add more time, 15 seconds at a time. Stir again. Can be reheated easily in the microwave, again at 70% power, 15 to 30 seconds at a time.

CHOCOLATE-LOVERS' COOKIE PIECRUST

*There are so many uses for this wonderful crust. Try it with **Ice Cream Social Pie** to start. Makes one 9-inch piecrust.*

20 cream-filled chocolate sandwich cookies
3 tablespoons melted butter or margarine
1 tablespoon **liqueur of choice***

Preheat oven to 350° F. Crush cookies by hand or in a food processor with a steel knife, until fine. Pour cookie crumbs into a 9-inch pie plate and drizzle with melted butter. Stir well to combine. Pat evenly to cover bottom and sides of pie plate. Bake for 10 to 12 minutes. Let cool slightly; drizzle liqueur over crust. Fill or refrigerate until ready to use.

Microwave Directions: Instead of baking, microwave crust on HIGH (100%) power for 2 to 2½ minutes, quarter-turn at 1 minute. Proceed as directed.

* **TIP:** Excellent liqueur choices for this recipe are: **Fresh Mint, Crème de Menthe, Amaretto, Hazelnut, Mexican Coffee** or **Old Jamaican Coffee.**

GOURMET FUDGE SAUCE

*Use on **Ice Cream Social Pie** or make wonderful gourmet ice cream sundaes. Using a food processor makes this recipe a snap. Makes about ¾ cup.*

4 ounces semi-sweet chocolate
¼ cup water
2 tablespoons butter or margarine
⅓ cup granulated cane sugar
2 tablespoons **liqueur of choice***

Insert steel knife/blade in food processor. Break chocolate blocks into smaller pieces. Turn processor on and drop pieces, one at a time, through feed tube. Process until finely minced. Heat water and butter; stir in sugar.

When sugar has dissolved, remove from heat and pour through feed tube with processor motor running. Add liqueur last. Sauce is ready for use.

* TIP: Excellent liqueur choices are: **Fresh Mint, Crème de Menthe, Amaretto, Hazelnut, Mexican Coffee, Old Jamaican Coffee,** or **Orange**.

ICE CREAM SOCIAL PIE

This pie has a rich, old-fashioned taste but is easy to make and freezes beautifully for "make-ahead" entertaining. Makes one 9-inch pie.

Fill **Chocolate-Lovers' Cookie Piecrust** with 1½ quarts French Vanilla or other favorite flavor ice cream. Place ice cream in scoops, slightly mounding up in the center. Set in freezer while making **Gourmet Fudge Sauce** (previous page). Pour completed fudge sauce over frozen ice cream pie. Return to freezer. **Whipped Liqueur Cream** (below) or conventional whipped cream maybe used to garnish this pie. Red or green maraschino cherries and/or chopped nuts make decorative additions to this dessert.

To make pie ahead, cover with plastic wrap or aluminum foil as soon as sauce has firmed in the freezer. Add whipped cream just before servmg.

WHIPPED LIQUEUR CREAM

*Use on **Ice Cream Social Pie** or any other recipe where a very special whipped cream is called for. Vary flavors to suit your recipe. Makes about 1 pint of whipped cream.*

½ pint (1 cup) whipping cream
2 to 3 tablespoons confectioners' cane sugar
1 tablespoon **liqueur of choice**

Whip cream until soft peaks form. Add sugar; whip a bit more. Add liqueur and whip lightly to combine. Serve or chill, covered, until needed.

DUTCH LAWYERS' PIE

A coconut crust, creamy filling with a surprise center layer combine to make this a spectacular pie! Makes one 9-inch pie.

Crust:
 ¼ cup melted butter or margarine
 2⅔ cups flaked sweetened coconut

Filling:
 ½ cup granulated cane sugar, divided
 1 envelope (1 tablespoon) unflavored gelatin
 3 eggs, separated
 ¾ cup milk
 ½ cup **Advocaat Liqueur**
 1 cup whipping cream
 1 teaspoon vanilla extract
 ½ teaspoon lemon extract
 whipped cream for garnish, if desired

Preheat oven to 325° F. In a medium saucepan, melt butter; stir in flaked coconut. Press half of this mixture over bottom and sides of a 9-inch pie plate. Spread remainder on a baking sheet. Bake both for 10 to 15 minutes, or until coconut is golden brown. (Watch closely! The coconut on the baking sheet may cook more quickly than the crust.) Remove from oven and let cool.

In medium saucepan, combine ¼ cup of the sugar, gelatin, egg yolks and milk. Stir constantly over medium low heat, until gelatin and sugar are dissolved. Cool to lukewarm; stir in the liqueur. Refrigerate until mixture is thick but not set.

In small mixing bowl, beat egg whites until soft peaks form. Add the remaining ¼ cup sugar gradually, while beating until stiff peaks form. Set aside. In a medium bowl, whip cream until stiff; gradually add vanilla and lemon extracts.

Fold the cream gently into the gelatin mixture, then fold in the beaten egg whites. Refrigerate until mixture holds its shape when mounded. Spoon half the filling into cooled crust. Layer with most of the toasted coconut. Top with remaining filling. Chill until set. Garnish with whipped cream and remaining toasted coconut. Serve chilled.

TRUFFLES

Rich chocolate and a mellow liqueur make an unbeatable combination in this special truffle recipe. Try **Mexican Coffee** *or* **Old Jamaican Coffee Liqueurs** *for Mocha Truffles. Other flavors that are heavenly with chocolate are* **Cherry, Orange, Raspberry, Hazelnut** *or* **Mint Liqueurs.** *You'll discover many favorites in this versatile recipe. Makes 1½ dozen large truffles.*

12 ounces semi-sweet chocolate, either chips or broken into pieces
4 tablespoons (1/2 stick) butter or margarine
¼ cup granulated cane sugar
2 egg yolks, beaten
1 cup finely chopped nuts (hazelnuts, pecans, walnuts or blanched almonds)
⅓ cup **liqueur of choice**
coating choice of: chocolate decorettes, unsweetened or pre-sweetened cocoa powder

Heat water in the bottom part of a double boiler. Place chocolate in the top half of the double boiler and stir until melted. Gradually stir in butter. Add sugar and continue to cook, stirring constantly until sugar is dissolved. Remove from heat and allow to cool as much as possible without letting chocolate harden. Quickly stir in beaten egg yolks. Add nuts and mix well. Stir in liqueur. Refrigerate 15 minutes or until mixture is easily handled and not sticky.

Place a small amount of your choice of coating in a small bowl. Shape refrigerated mixture into large balls (about 1¼-inch). Roll in coating. Chill until very firm.

LIGHT RASPBERRY FROST

An elegant and light dessert. Refreshingly perfect! Serve in chilled stemmed glasses. Makes five servings.

1(10-ounce) package sweetened frozen raspberries, thawed
1 tablespoon cornstarch
¼ cup confectioners' cane sugar
¼ cup **Raspberry Liqueur**
few additional fresh or frozen berries

Place a small strainer over a glass measuring cup. Drain juice off raspberries through strainer. Measure juice; add water, if necessary, to equal ½ cup. Combine 2 tablespoons juice and cornstarch in a small bowl; set aside.

In a small saucepan combine remaining juice and sugar. Cook over low heat, stirring to dissolve sugar. Add reserved cornstarch mixture and continue stirring until mixture is thick and clear. Add Raspberry Liqueur and stir in thawed berries. Spoon into serving dishes. Top with additional berries if desired.

Microwave Directions: To quickly thaw frozen berries, place unopened paper box on plate and microwave on DEFROST (30%) power for 3 to 5 minutes, then let stand 5 minutes. If top of container is metal, remove top as directed and place container, open side up, on a plate and microwave as directed.

Follow recipe directions, but combine juice and sugar in a microwave-safe medium mixing bowl. Microwave on HIGH (100%) power for 1 minute, stirring once. Add cornstarch mixture, stirring in well. Continue microwaving on HIGH for 2 to 3 minutes, stirring every minute, until mixture is thick and clear. Follow remaining directions above.

MELON SORBET

A refreshing and light sorbet with just a touch of liqueur from one of our favorite cooks, Janice Kenyon. She is the author of **Light Fantastic: Health-Conscious Entertaining** *cookbook. Serves 6 to 8.*

Purée in food processor:
chunks of 4 small or 3 medium cantaloupe or other sweet melon, peeled and seeded, enough to make about 4 cups purée (save some melon balls for garnish)

Add:
½ cup water
3 tablespoons honey
juice of 1 lime
2 tablespoons fruit liqueur, preferably **Raspberry Liqueur**

Garnish:
melon balls, same or different type of melon strawberries (optional)
kiwi fruit slices (optional)

Pour mixture into 2 freezer trays or 9 x 9-inch baking pan and freeze until firm, about 1 hour. Remove from freezer, break into chunks and process in food processor until smooth. Freeze again and repeat blending process two more times (an ice cream maker does these steps automatically). Transfer from freezer to refrigerator while dinner is being served.

To serve, scoop into small serving bowls over a few melon balls (another kind of melon for contrast if desired), and garnish with a whole strawberry and/or slice of kiwi fruit.

ELEGANT BERRY WHIP

Serve icy cold in stemmed glasses. A wide variety of berries may be used with this recipe. Raspberries and strawberries are two favorites. Serves 6.

    2 cups (1 pint) fresh berries
    1 cup whipping cream
    ½ cup sifted confectioners' cane sugar
    1 egg white
    1 tablespoon **liqueur of choice***

Prepare berries; wash, remove hulls, etc. Set aside 6 whole, perfect berries. Place remaining berries in blender or food processor and purée.

Whip cream until soft peaks form, then beat in sugar. Beat egg white until stiff. Fold beaten egg white gently into fruit purée. Fold purée mixture into cream mixture. Spoon into six individual dishes or stemmed glasses. Chill well. Garnish with reserved berries.

***Raspberry, Strawberry, Lemon,** or **Amaretto Liqueurs** are very good in this recipe.

QUICK BLUEBERRY DELIGHT

A simple dessert or brunch dish that is quick to prepare and delightful to eat. Serves 1; increase as needed for quantity.

    ½ cup fresh or thawed frozen blueberries
    1 tablespoon any **Orange Liqueur**
    1 heaping tablespoon whipped cream or **Whipped Liqueur Cream**

In dessert bowl place washed, drained blueberries. Spoon liqueur over berries and let stand at least 5 minutes. Top with whipped cream of choice just before serving.

STRAWBERRY ICE

This easy, light and luscious recipe can be made with any of our **Orange Liqueurs.** *Fellow author Janice Kenyon shares this outstanding example of a liqueur-enhanced dessert from her* **Light Fantastic: Health-Conscious Entertaining** *cookbook. Serves 4 to 6.*

Purée in blender or food processor:
   2 cups sliced strawberries, fresh or thawed frozen
   1 tablespoon lemon juice

In medium saucepan combine purée with:
   1¾ cups water
   ½ cup cane sugar

Heat to boiling and boil slowly until frothy, about 5 minutes.

Add:
   3 tablespoons **Orange Liqueur**

Pour into freezer tray and freeze until slushy firm, about 2 hours. Remove from freezer tray, beat to break up chunks if necessary.

Then fold in:

1 stiffly beaten egg white

Return to freezer until firm, about 1 hour. Serve garnished with sliced berries or kiwi fruit.

SUMMER FRUIT CREAM

*These cool and luscious desserts are easy to put together having just three ingredients. Mix and match to the season and your taste. Here are some combinations to get you started: raspberries with **Raspberry Liqueur**, peaches with **Peach Liqueur**, or pineapple chunks with **Hawaiian Fruit Liqueur**. An excellent make-ahead dessert for impromptu entertaining. Increase recipe as needed. Serves 2.*

1 cup prepared fresh fruit
¼ cup **fruit liqueur of choice**
⅓ cup or 1 scoop vanilla pudding or ice cream

Prepare fruit, wash, pit or cut as necessary into bite size pieces and place in bowl. Pour liqueur over fruit, cover and chill. To serve, place pudding or ice cream in individual bowls and spoon cup liqueured fruit around, drizzle some liqueur on top of pudding or ice cream.

CHOCOLATE CHERRY CREAM

Summer fruit and rich chocolate—simple and deliciously decadent. This is a perfect make-ahead dessert for company that can be quickly assembled. Increase recipe as needed. Serves 2.

1 cup pitted and halved sweet cherries
¼ Cup **Cherry Liqueur**
¼ cup **Gourmet Fudge Sauce** (page 152)
⅓ cup or 1 scoop chocolate pudding or ice cream

Prepare cherries and place in bowl. Pour liqueur over cherries, cover and chill. Warm pre-prepared **Gourmet Fudge Sauce**. To serve, place pudding or ice cream into individual bowls and spoon ½ cup liqueured fruit around; drizzle cup fudge sauce over each serving.

STEAMED ORANGE PUDDING

Moist, cake-like steamed puddings are an English favorite. Make them without any special equipment using our quick "oven-steaming" method. Try this homey, old-fashioned dessert served warm and topped with a custard sauce or our special **California Lemon Sauce** *(page 166). Serves 6.*

½ cup Sultana raisins
¼ cup dark raisins
¼ cup any type of **Orange Liqueur**
1 cup dry bread crumbs
¾ cup all-purpose flour
⅓ cup brown cane sugar
½ cup granulated cane sugar
1 teaspoon freshly grated orange peel
½ teaspoon freshly grated lemon peel
1 teaspoon baking soda
¼ cup scalded milk
¼ cup cold milk
½ cup (1 stick) butter or margarine, melted
1 beaten egg
2 to 3 tablespoons **any citrus liqueur**

Preheat oven to 375° F. Measure raisins; pour the ¼ cup liqueur over them. Set aside until needed. Mix bread crumbs, flour, sugars, orange and lemon peels in a large mixing bowl, stirring Until well mixed. Stir baking soda into the scalded milk, then add remaining milk. Stir in melted butter and beaten egg. Pour into crumb-flour mixture; mixing well. Stir in the raisin-liqueur mixture. Butter a 1-quart baking dish. Spoon batter into dish. Cover with aluminum foil, sealing down all around. Pour about ¾ inch of water into a cake pan; place the 1-quart baking dish into cake pan. Set carefully into oven. Bake 1¼ hours. Test center with a toothpick (will come out clean when done). When cool, drizzle with your choice of a citrus liqueur.

WHITE CHOCOLATE HAZELNUT HEAVEN

*This versatile recipe can be served as a fondue, used as a drizzle topping or when allowed to harden, a confection. **Hazelnut Liqueur,** our version of Frangelico, is used in this recipe. May be made ahead for entertaining, refrigerate or freeze. Makes about 4 cups.*

> 3 cups (14 ounces) white chocolate chips or finely chopped white chocolate
> ¾ cup whipping cream or half and half
> 1 tablespoon **Hazelnut Liqueur**
> ½ teaspoon vanilla extract
> ½ cup finely chopped toasted hazelnuts (also known as "filberts")

Microwave Directions: Put white chocolate into a 2-quart microwave safe bowl. Microwave chocolate on HIGH (100 %) power for 1 minute. Set aside.

Pour cream into a 1-cup glass measure and microwave on HIGH power for 1 to 1½ minutes or just until cream reaches a boil. While cream is heating, stir chocolate with a whisk to smooth. Pour hot cream over melted chocolate, whisk to combine. Stir in liqueur and vanilla, then hazelnuts.

For immediate use: Pour into container(s) or may be refrigerated up to 4 weeks.

For future use: Freeze, leaving ½-inch headspace in freezer container.

For fondue: Pour finished recipe into fondue dish, keep warm over flame, stir occasionally. Serve with assorted fresh fruits or firm cake such as pound or angel food for dipping.

For confection: Dip fruit with stems, such as cherries or strawberries, into fondue and place on waxed paper laid on a plate or tray. Refrigerate. Serve chilled fruit confection. Or pour finished recipe into square pan, cover and refrigerate. Cut into squares when set up.

For drizzling: Design a large fruit plate and drizzle desired amount of warm recipe over fruit. Allow guests to help themselves.

VARIATION:

WHITE CHOCOLATE ALMOND HEAVEN: Substitute chopped toasted almonds for hazelnuts and **Amaretto Liqueur** for the **Hazelnut Liqueur.** Prepare as directed.

VANILLA SUGAR

Excellent for desserts, coffees and confections. A good way to make full use of expensive vanilla beans used in liqueur making. Makes 2 cups.

Rinse vanilla beans in cool water to remove any liqueur. Place on a doubled paper towel and pat tops dry with another paper towel. Let dry completely.

When dry, place in a pint jar with two cups granulated sugar, cap and shake well. Let age at least a few days before using.

STAR OF THE BACKYARD BARBECUE SAUCE

*Here's a nice, perky sauce that works well with chicken, beef or pork. Fruit liqueurs are best in this recipe and we like to use **Tony's Key Lime**, any **Orange, Citrus, Plum** or **Cherry Liqueur**. Makes 2 cups, but you may want to double the recipe, since it freezes well.*

> 2 pounds fresh tomatoes (about 3 to 4 large), peeled
> 1 medium sweet onion, peeled
> 6 cloves garlic, peeled
> ¼ teaspoon ground allspice
> ¼ teaspoon ground cloves
> ¼ teaspoon ground cinnamon
> ½ teaspoon salt
> ½ teaspoon freshly ground pepper
> ¼ teaspoon celery seed
> 2 teaspoons olive or canola oil
> 2 teaspoons Worcestershire sauce
> 2 tablespoons brown cane sugar
> ½ cup **any fruit liqueur**

Cut tomatoes and onions into fourths. In a food processor, purée tomatoes, onions and garlic until smooth. Place in medium saucepan. Add spices, oil and Worcestershire sauce. Bring to a boil, stirring constantly. Reduce heat to medium-low until a slow simmer is maintained. Simmer, uncovered, stirring frequently for 25 minutes. Sauce will thicken.

Add brown sugar and liqueur; stir to blend well. Continue simmering, stirring often for an additional 5 minutes. Sauce may be used immediately, or stored in an airtight container. refrigerated and/or frozen.

AMARETTO APPLESAUCE

A fresh sauce that is excellent over gingerbread or as a filling for dessert crêpes. Top with a dusting of confectioners' sugar, sour or whipped cream for a finishing touch. Wonderful with pork too. Microwave cooking experts Joyce Webster and Susan Vander Velde share this from their great dessert cookbook, **Try It, You'll Like It! Microwaved Desserts.** *Makes 2 cups.*

4 apples, peeled and cored
2 tablespoons butter
½ cup cane sugar
1 teaspoon grated orange rind
2 tablespoons orange juice
1 egg, separated
2 tablespoons **Amaretto Liqueur**

Chop apples and combine with butter, sugar, orange rind and juice in a 4-cup mixing bowl. Microwave on HIGH power for 5 minutes, uncovered or cook conventionally until apples are tender. Stir once or twice. Purée apples in food processor or blender.

Beat egg yolk and liqueur together. Add to applesauce. Whip egg white until stiff. Gradually blend into applesauce.

CALIFORNIA LEMON SAUCE

A bright and sunny sauce that has so many uses. Wonderful over plum pudding, gingerbread, pound cake or our **Steamed Orange Pudding** (see page 161). Makes about 1 cup.

¾ cup water
½ cup granulated cane sugar
2 tablespoons cornstarch
1 tablespoon butter
¼ cup lemon juice, fresh preferred
2 teaspoons grated fresh lemon rind
1 egg, beaten
2 tablespoons **Lemon Liqueur**

Bring water to a boil. In a small saucepan, combine sugar and cornstarch. Gradually stir in boiling water. Boil 1 minute, stirring constantly.

Remove from heat and stir in butter, lemon juice and rind. Gradually blend in egg and finally liqueur. Serve slightly warm or cool.

CRANBERRY JEWELS IN LIQUEUR

The colors are beautiful in this memorable side dish that is especially good with poultry. Makes a lovely gourmet gift. Makes about 1 quart.

1 cup granulated cane sugar
½ cup orange juice
2 cups cranberries
½ cup any **Orange Liqueur**
1 can (11 ounces) mandarin oranges, well-drained

Combine sugar and orange juice in a large saucepan. Cook over medium heat, about 3 to 4 minutes, stirring occasionally until sugar dissolves. Stir in cranberries. Heat to boiling point then reduce heat. Simmer uncovered until juice is released from cranberries, about 10 minutes. Add liqueur and mandarin oranges; simmer 2 minutes. Pour into container, cool, cover and refrigerate. Serve chilled.

Microwave Directions: In a 1½ to 2-quart microwavable bowl, combine sugar, orange juice and cranberries. Cover and microwave on HIGH power for 3 minutes. Stir and microwave for 2 to 3 minutes more, or until cranberries have popped their skins. Let stand covered, for 5 minutes. Gently stir in liqueur and drained mandarin oranges. Cover and refrigerate. Serve chilled.

GOLDEN CREAM

*True Galliano lovers will be delighted with this recipe. It blends our **Italiano Gold Liqueur** with fresh pineapple and creamed cheese for an unique topping or dip, Try it spooned over pound or tea cake, dip homemade doughnuts or beignets into it, or spread it on French toast, waffles or hot bran muffins. Makes about 2 cups.*

½ cup (1 stick) unsalted butter
8 ounces (1 large package) cream cheese
1 cup confectioners' cane sugar
2 tablespoons **Italiano Gold Liqueur**
¾ cup fresh pineapple chunks*

Cut butter and cream cheese into chunks. Place in food processor work bowl fitted with steel knife. Add confectioners' sugar and process until mixture is creamed. Add liqueur and pulse to combine. Add pineapple chunks and process by pulsing off and on until pineapple is in small chunks and mixture is well combined.

Alternate method: If preferred, use a hand or electric mixer to make this recipe. Cut pineapple chunks smaller and stir into creamed mixture.

*NOTE: Fresh pineapple is preferred but pineapple canned in natural juice may be substituted. Drain well before use.

LIQUEURED FRUIT SAUCE

A quick, easy and gourmet sauce that can be spooned over almost anything!
Makes even plain pound cake, bread pudding or vanilla ice cream sing! Good
make-ahead recipe. Makes about ¾ cup.

    1 teaspoon fresh orange or lemon zest
    1 cup apricot, peach or mango preserves
    5 tablespoons **Apricot, Peach** or **Tropical Mango Liqueur,** divided

Combine zest, preserves and 2 tablespoons liqueur in a small saucepan.
Heat to a boil, stirring constantly. Reduce heat and simmer gently for about
10 minutes, stirring frequently. Remove from heat and stir in 3 tablespoons
liqueur. Serve slightly warm.

Refrigerate any leftover sauce. Reheats easily.

ORIENTAL PLUM SAUCE

Another one of our students' cooking class favorites. It is an exotic cousin of Sweet and Sour sauce. Its rich, fruity taste combines plums and apricots with the added pizzazz of **Orange Liqueur.** *Choose any of the* **Orange Liqueurs,** *including* **Taboo,** *in this book; all are successful in this recipe. Serve with meats or poultry. Especially good as a dipping sauce for fried won ton, Chinese chicken wings or egg rolls. Makes about 1½ cups.*

¼ cup dried apricots
boiling water
1 cup fresh or frozen pitted red or purple plums*
2 tablespoons plum juice or water
½ cup granulated cane sugar*
½ teaspoon dry powdered mustard
⅛ teaspoon white or black pepper
¼ cup white vinegar or white wine vinegar
¼ cup **Orange Liqueur**

Cover dried apricots with boiling water and let stand 10 minutes. Drain and finely chop apricots by hand or in a food processor with a steel knife/blade. Finely chop plums. Place fruit in a medium saucepan; add the 2 tablespoons juice or water. Bring just to a boil, lower heat and simmer for 15 minutes, stirring frequently.

Add sugar, mustard and pepper. Simmer for 10 minutes. Stir in vinegar. Simmer 5 minutes. Remove from heat and cool to lukewarm. Stir in liqueur. Serve at room temperature or slightly warmed.

Microwave Directions: Prepare fruit as directed. Omit any additional juice or water from recipe. Place fruit in a small glass mixing bowl and microwave on HIGH power, stirring after 2 minutes; stir. Reduce power to MEDIUM-LOW (50%) power and simmer 5 minutes. Stir every minute.

Add sugar and spices, mixing well. Simmer for 4 minutes on MEDIUM-LOW (30%) power, stirring after 2 minutes. Let cool and stir in liqueur. Serve as directed.

*NOTE: One 16-ounce can of drained and pitted purple plums may be substituted for the fresh or frozen plums. Decrease sugar to ¼ cup. Check consistency, juice or water may not be necessary.

LIME MARINADE

For salmon steaks broiled or grilled to perfection, try marinating them first for at least 1 hour in this remarkable marinade. You'll find it's also excellent for marinating sliced meat for fajitas. This recipe is sufficient to marinate 4 to 5 salmon steaks.

½ cup **Lime Liqueur** or **Tony's Key Lime Liqueur**
¼ cup olive oil
1 lime or 2 Key limes, sliced
4 cloves garlic, crushed
½ teaspoon salt
¼ teaspoon freshly ground black pepper

Combine all ingredients in a 1-gallon bag with a zipped lock.

For salmon steaks, marinate right in the bag. Simply add salmon, seal bag, squeezing out air, and refrigerate for at least one hour, turning bag over occasionally. Cook as desired.

HIGHLAND MARMALADE

Put some of this marmalade on a hot scone, take a bite and close your eyes. You can almost feel the Scottish mist curl at your feet and smell the heather in bloom. Top a jar with a piece of tartan fabric for a perfect gift to any marmalade or Drambuie lover. Makes seven 6-ounce jars.

  4 large, sweet oranges (Valencia or other sweet variety)
  1 medium lemon, Meyer lemon preferred
  8 cups water
  2¾ cups water
  8 cups granulated cane sugar
  ½ cup **Scottish Highland Liqueur**

Wash oranges and lemon. Trim ends and cut into quarters. Remove and discard all seeds. Thinly shred oranges and lemon by hand or with a shredding disc in food processor. (May be thinly sliced if preferred.) Pour shredded fruit and accumulated juice into a large glass or ceramic bowl(s), add 8 cups water. Cover and let stand 24 hours.

Remove any large pieces of improperly cut rind and fruit membrane. Pour shredded fruit and juice into an 8-quart or larger saucepan or canning kettle. Add remaining 2¾ cups water and bring mixture to a boil. Turn heat down so that a low boil is maintained.

Stir in sugar and continue stirring gently until sugar has dissolved. Continue the low boil, stirring occasionally until marmalade is well reduced and forms a firm jelly when tested. Begin to test the marmalade 30 minutes after the sugar has been added. Test either with a cooking thermometer (should reach 225° F) or with a spoon (marmalade should "sheet" when a small quantity is poured off the side of a spoon).

When the correct stage has been reached, turn off burner and stir in Scottish Highland Liqueur. Let marmalade sit for 10 minutes before ladling into hot, sterilized jelly jars; seal.

Hints and Tips for Cooking with Liqueurs

Herbal liqueurs usually have strong flavors and should be used sparingly in food or cocktail recipes.

Crème de Menthe Liqueur and rice vinegar, in equal portions or to taste, make a refreshing dressing drizzled lightly over a fruit salad. Substitute other liqueurs for new and different flavor treats.

A special seafood butter sauce can be made by combining melted butter and a dash or two of **Anisette Liqueur.**

Use liqueurs much as you would extracts. Substitute a couple of tablespoons of **Crème de Menthe, Coffee** or **Orange Liqueur** for some of the water in your next chocolate cake for a surprising change.

Pour a favorite **fruit liqueur** over a grapefruit half for a special treat.

The easiest sundae of all: vanilla ice cream and **your favorite liqueur.** Also good topped with liqueured fruits and liqueur.

To flambé a dish with a liqueur, warm the liqueur gently for 1 minute in the pan then ignite it carefully with a match. Or warm in the microwave. Place ⅓ cup liqueur in glass measuring cup and microwave on HIGH power 15 seconds.

Add a can of drained mandarin oranges to any **Orange Liqueur** after the first straining. Age and strain as directed. Save oranges and top a cheese cake with fruit and drizzled liqueur.

Add a couple of tablespoons of **Apple Liqueur** to your next apple, apple-berry, mince, quince or raisin pie for great flavor.

Baste your next roast turkey with an **Orange** or **Cranberry Liqueur** for unique flavor.

Citrus liqueurs are especially versatile for cooking. Drizzle over fruits for a special fruit cup or light dessert.

Herbal liqueurs have historically been used for medicinal purposes. A tablespoon or two in fruit juice or hot tea or in a small liqueur glass to sip are common dosages.

ABOUT THE AUTHORS

Oregonians Cheryl Long and Heather Kibbey have shared a long-time friendship, even before the days when they were food columnists for the Lake Oswego (Oregon) Review, subsequent editors-in-chief of Oregon Restaurateur magazine, and co-authors of *How to Make A World of Liqueurs* (1984). Cheryl, a home economist, had previously written the book, *How to Make and Cook with Danish Liqueurs* (1983).

Each went on to write many more books, but who could have guessed that, thirty years later, the two original liqueur books (which they soon merged into one volume, **Classic Liqueurs**), would have become the definitive guide to the art of making liqueurs in the home kitchen.

Their Junior Dessert–Testing Panel members (aka their kids) have grown, with children of their own. Yet the authors continue to explore the world of liqueurs and are only too happy when called upon by the publisher for another update!

INDEX

Classic Liqueurs:
The Fine Art of Creating, Re-creating, and Cooking with Liqueurs

is available internationally
in bookstores and culinary shops,
or may be purchased online
through Amazon.com

Published by:
Panoply Press
PO Box 1885
Lake Oswego, OR 97035

PanoplyPress@gmail.com

Made in the USA
Charleston, SC
27 October 2015